Healing Cancer without Drugs

One Day at a Time

Rhona Byrne

Medical Disclaimer

The information contained in this book is provided for education. It is not intended as, and should not be relied upon as, medical advice. The publisher and author is not responsible for any specific health needs that may require medical supervision. If you have any underlying health problems or have any doubts about the advice contained in this book, you should contact a qualified medical, dietary, or other appropriate professional.

The Solopreneur Publishing Company Ltd focuses on the needs of each individual author client. This book has been published through their 'Solopreneur Self-Publishing (SSP)' brand that enables authors to have complete control over their finished book whilst utilising the expert advice and services usually reserved for traditionally published print, in order to produce an attractive, engaging, quality product. Please note, however, that final editorial decisions and approval rested with the author. The publisher takes no responsibility for the accuracy of the content.

ISBN 978-09957520-7-8

Printed in the U.K.

CONTENTS

Dedication

I dedicate this book to my two wonderful daughters, Caitlin and Melissa. For your belief in, and total acceptance of what your 'rather crazy' mum was doing to heal herself. Your love and encouragement never outwardly wavered. I feel truly blessed to have two such strong, loving and courageous teenagers in my life. You were, and will continue to be my inspiration, always.

Acknowledgements

First, I would like to thank my family for helping me see through my unconventional healing journey.

In particular, I want to mention John who, despite our differing opinion on occasions, listened to my ongoing saga, and contributed practically where he could. Then, when the positive results came thorough, for accepting, gracefully, that I had taken the right path.

Thank you again to my girls, Caitlin and Melissa for the trust they had in me, from day one.

Thank you to my mum, who has since passed on to the next world. I know you will understand why I was unable to tell you about my diagnosis. I simply did not want you to worry about me. You are free now to watch and enjoy the family from a place of peace.

Dad, you were my inspiration when I was growing up. I always remember how you taught me that if someone else could do it, then I could too if I wanted to. This belief helped me to see past the rhetoric of the doctors. To embrace the positive stories of others who had survived cancer, following a plethora of different unconventional routes.

Thanks also to my sister, for her calls and words of support from across the world. It was great to chat on a regular basis with someone so close, who has known me all my life.

I also wish to thank all of John's family, for their belief in me and what I was doing. In particular, his mum Philo, brother Charles, and sister Yvonne, for their practical suggestions and kind words.

I am also indebted to all my close friends and spiritual buddies for their helpful suggestions, and unwavering acknowledgement of my sometimes 'weird and whacky' alternative treatments. They became my truly unconventional healing support groups.

Rosa Hughes, from Medical Thermal Imaging – thank you for sharing the story of your own healing journey with John, and helping to convince him that what I was doing was not "completely crazy". Thank you also for giving me the metaphorical 'kick up the backside' that I needed to get my book published, by asking Gail Powell to give me a call.

And to Gail herself, a big thank you for your help in making this book a reality.

Finally, thank **you** for showing an interest in my book, and allowing me to share the story of my healing journey with you. I sincerely hope that there is something within the pages which can help to inspire and motivate you and your loved ones.

What is love?

It is all around us; Just there for the taking, and for the giving.

Where do I begin with my story? Is it really just my story?

Prologue

*The butterfly counts not months but moments
and has time enough.*

Rabindranath Tagore

The purpose of this book is for me to share my healing story with those who are interested. I am not telling other people to do what I have done. What I am doing is simply letting those who are interested know that there are other options available. I know and respect many people who have chosen to take the advice of medical experts and follow the medicinal route.

There are many success stories for both conventional and alternative approaches. There are also people who have employed a combination of both. Perhaps opting for surgery, but refusing chemotherapy and radiotherapy.

I do believe, however, that for those who opt for conventional treatment, their bodies have a much harder job to eliminate all the toxins with which they are bombarded. I am also aware that some of those who choose a different path from what the medical professionals advise do not survive for a variety of reasons.

I discovered a great deal during my own journey and in talking to others who have been diagnosed with cancer about their individual journeys. This has led me to the conclusion that belief is such an important part of the healing process. As such, if someone believes that they will get better, they have a much greater chance than those who live in fear. I am also certain that the emotional causes of illness need to be addressed in some way. Therefore, dealing with emotions such as anger, resentment and fear also help to heal our bodies.

In summary, I believe that healing is really about loving oneself on every level. This is about loving and respecting our bodies by nourishing them with positive self-talk, good food, and moderate exercise. To do this, it is important to truly listen to the body and what it needs at all times. From my experience, dealing with repressed emotional memories helps to set us free. Discovering our spiritual side helps us to live in peace with who we truly are. Finding out what we enjoy and enabling ourselves to have fun is vitally important for our wellbeing, as is not taking ourselves too seriously. I have learned to relish every precious moment of each day. With all its multitude of challenges and blessings, this is definitely part of the panacea for a happy, healthy life.

I sincerely hope that this book is an inspiration to those who read my very personal story.

Much love and many blessings

Rhona Byrne

Chapter 1

"Oh my God, what am I going to do?"

This being human is hard sometimes.

It was the 8th of September 2015, and I had just been told by a rather large, bespectacled consultant, that I *probably have cancer!!* The word CANCER applied to me? It felt surreal somehow, as if the statement applied to the person in my body, but I seemed to be viewing myself from a distance asking; *Is that diagnosis really for me?*

What was my worst fear? At this stage, it was the prospect of telling my husband John and my two beautiful girls, Caitlin and Melissa. I could feel the panic rise in me as I tried to contemplate what I was going to say. I knew it would be the most difficult conversation I had ever had. How could I put into words, what I knew in my heart to be true?

No one had known that I was going to the hospital that day for a check-up, just as I hadn't confided in anyone. I had visited the doctor one month earlier, as I had suspected something was wrong. There was no identifiable lump; I just had a feeling that something was not quite right. I was now wishing; *perhaps I should have said something to John?*

Out of nowhere, it dawned on me that hindsight is the arch-enemy of rational thought, so I tried to overcome the negativity in my mind. At the time, I had been hoping that everything would all be okay and that I would be given the all-clear by the doctors.

The last thing I wanted to do was worry John or anyone else unnecessarily. After all, I had had similar check-ups before which turned out to be false alarms. Five years previously I had found a lump in my breast which turned out to be a benign cyst. I remember the feeling of relief when the doctor had told me. On that occasion, I was overjoyed at the outcome.

This time, I hadn't found a lump as such, there was a slight pulling of the skin on my left breast. That was all the physical evidence I had. Deep down, however, I had a feeling that something was not right. My general health was not good, as I'd been suffering increasingly from exhaustion the proceeding few months. There didn't seem to be any real explanation for the way I was feeling. I'd also developed a dry, raspy, unexplained cough which had lasted a few weeks. The cough was so bad, in fact, I had been experiencing more frequent coughing fits which literally took my breath away; so much so that I felt that I couldn't breathe. Yes, I just *knew* something was wrong!

I had visited various GPs over the prior few months who didn't seem to think that there was anything wrong with me. On a recent visit, I had been prescribed antibiotics for my cough, although there was no real proof that I had an ailment which could be alleviated by taking these pills.

The difficult thing was that although the doctors appeared to be well-meaning, I found no consistency with the care I received from my GP's practice. The days of the *family doctor* who gets to know his or her patients seem to be long gone. This traditional approach has been replaced by a system more geared towards processing patients and meeting targets, rather than really getting to know patients; resulting in a reduced emphasis on advising patients specifically for their personal requirements.

The GP I saw when I enquired about my breast abnormality was an Asian doctor of stocky build and direct manner, who had an eager young female trainee with him. He asked if it was okay if the student doctor examined me too. As I had no objection, they both examined my breasts. Afterwards, as I was sitting on the crumpled paper covering the examination couch, buttoning up my blouse, I heard them discussing my case from the other side of the curtain.

In her eagerness to impress, the student was explaining that as she could not feel a lump, why would the GP refer me to a consultant for further investigation? He explained that anyone coming with a suspected problem with their breasts is automatically referred, even if there are no obvious signs that there is a problem. I stood up noisily and pulled back the curtain, cutting short any further explanation he may have had for the student, as I was keen to know how soon I would be seen by a consultant. The GP looked directly at me over his glasses; his confidence enforcing the fact that he had certainly done this many times before. Explaining that he couldn't feel a lump, therefore I probably had nothing to worry about. He said he would, however, refer me to the hospital for further checks, as is the correct protocol when someone has concerns about unusual lumps or other changes in their breasts.

It didn't surprise me that neither the GP nor the eager student could detect anything abnormal. I knew there was no obvious lump. I just instinctively felt that something wasn't as it should be. Momentarily I wondered, *why are women told to check for lumps?* At that precise time, it seemed absurd as I wouldn't be having any checks if I had been waiting until I found a lump! The GP continued to explain that he was going to refer me for further tests, and enquired which hospital would I prefer to go to? As I didn't really have a preference at that time, I opted for the one I thought would be the easiest to drive to from my house.

I mistakenly assumed that my appointment for further

checks would be relatively quick, and at least within a week of my visit to the doctor. I was disappointed when I had to wait two weeks for an appointment to be seen by a consultant at the hospital. At the time, I saw this as being detrimental to my situation. As time went on, I knew it was beneficial to me when I decided to follow an alternative route to the one prescribed by the hospital consultant. I wasn't in that place yet, so every day I had to wait seemed to drag. It was difficult to focus on anything else other than the fact that I knew there was something very wrong happening within my body.

Eventually, the day of my initial consultation at the hospital arrived. As I sat alone in the waiting room known as the Jasmine Suite, I could feel the tension rising in me. My heart was beating so hard in my chest; I was sure the other people sitting in the waiting area could hear it.

Using my mindfulness training, I tried hard to focus on my breathing. Consciously observing each breath as it entered and exited my lungs, feeling my abdomen expanding and contracting. Continuously bringing myself back to the present moment was helping me deal with the situation I found myself in. I admit it is hard to practise mindfulness when in the throes of a crisis, so I tried some self-talk by explaining to myself at that moment; *I can do this. This is what I know, and this is what I teach.* Forcing myself to smile, as I sat there. Focussing my mind on carrying out an energy healing meditation, using another of my skills to help me keep calm.

"Rhona Byrne," the nurse's shrill voice called out. My peace was shattered. *It's my turn,* I acknowledged to myself. I waved my hand briefly at the nurse, who was standing looking around the room expectantly. Taking a moment to gather my thoughts, I collected my belongings from the seat next to me. Slightly flustered, I fumbled clumsily as I attempted to pick up my coat and handbag. Sombrely I stood up and followed the short, friendly looking nurse into one of the consulting rooms.

Walking through the door, I saw a rather plump consultant sitting at his desk in front of a computer screen. He was looking at some notes within a folder open in front of him. As I entered, he looked up from the paperwork and smiled at me. "Please take a seat, Mrs. Byrne". I remember thinking that his jovial manner belied the fact that he was a breast cancer specialist.

To me, the consultant's demeanour seemed extraordinarily jovial, and at odds with how I was feeling. He proceeded to converse with me in an upbeat manner during my examination. After which he casually announced that he could not feel any lump in my left breast, apart from what seemed like some cysts. He said that he would nevertheless send me downstairs to the x-ray department for further tests.

Form in hand detailing his prognosis and what further tests I required, I proceeded downstairs to another waiting room. I was to have a mammogram. This was to be the third mammogram I had experienced, so I was aware of what to expect. However, if I had known then what I now know about the dangers of mammography, I would never have agreed to such a barbaric, invasive test. Because the breasts are squashed to give a better image, the amount of ionising radiation experienced is deemed to be much worse than a normal x-ray. In addition, if the person has a tumour, crushing may make it spread. This topic is covered in detail in a book by Ty Bollinger called 'The Truth About Cancer'.[1] Although I was unaware of the potential risks of mammography, I did remember something I had read about the dangers of radiation to the throat whilst undergoing a mammogram.

Just as I was being led through to where the procedure would take place, I remembered to ask for a throat shield. The officious nurse didn't like my request at all, asking in a condescending tone "why do you want one of those?" and further proclaiming "I don't think we have one." I was not deterred and responded confidently, my tone belying the fear I felt inside, "I won't have the mammogram unless I can have a shield to protect my throat." At which point she disappeared for one or two minutes, returning with the required throat shield in her hand. Passing it to me without making eye contact. *Oh God,* I could feel the muscles in my stomach constrict as I thought, *This is not a good start.*

Next, the nurse proceeded to position my breasts on the cold white plate which was going to squeeze them during the procedure. It took me all my willpower at that moment to hold in the scream which was halted in my throat, as first my left then my right breast was compressed by the contraption. Initially from the top and bottom and then from each side. Holding each breast in position long enough for the x-rays to be taken.

I resorted to holding my breath on each occasion, whilst willing it to be over as quickly as possible. The machine refused to cooperate with my request. It crushed each breast in turn in the various painful positions, then proceeded to bombard them with radiation. Finally, just as I felt I would explode from holding in the feelings of agony, I was freed from the contraption. Taking a few deep breaths, I covered my naked body once more in the scratchy, blue and white cotton hospital gown.

As I sat in the corridor after my ordeal, I did wonder why women are subjected to such barbaric tests, and if they are necessary to give an accurate diagnosis. I now believe that mammography should be banned due to the dangers it poses. Finally, after what seemed like a long wait but in real time was probably only ten minutes, I was then ushered into another room for an ultrasound scan.

This scan was carried out by a rather brusque ultrasound technician, who gave the distinct impression of superiority. He didn't explain much to me as he did the scan, despite my feeble attempts at small talk. However, once he had studied the screen in front of him and referred to my notes, he then announced in his superior tone that he wanted to give me a biopsy. Going on to explain that he wanted to check a suspicious dark lump in my left breast. It had been detected on the x-ray and had also been picked up on the ultrasound. The shock of his proclamation reverberated through my body as if someone had punched me in the stomach.

"Will it be painful?" I enquired in a voice not much more than a whisper. *Oh God, this is not good* my mind was screaming in my head. In a tone, I can only describe as sarcastic, the brusque ultrasound technician exclaimed: "As I have never experienced the procedure myself, I couldn't say!" I could feel the panic rise from the pit of my stomach. *Breathe* I was commanding myself. *Just keep breathing, and it will be okay,* my thoughts tried to reassure me, but I wasn't able to convince myself. There was an involuntary tremble rippling through my body. It felt like my whole destiny was now out of my control. Trying to compose myself, I enquired shakily, "Will I be told the results afterwards?"

"The cells removed during the biopsy will be tested to check if enough of them have been taken to provide a clear diagnosis," came the reply.

Once again, I could hear the superiority in the ultrasound technician's voice. This man exuded confidence. He knew what was right. Unfortunately, I didn't share his confidence. I could feel my resolve slowly crumbling. *Just breathe, Rhona,* my inner voice was still trying hard to keep me in check. Further explanation from the ultrasound technician gave me my answer.

"The cells will have to be tested to see if they are cancerous, and the results will not be available today."

I was given a brief injection of local anaesthetic followed, rather too quickly for my liking, by one of the most excruciatingly painful assaults on my body that I had experienced. I screamed out in shock as the biopsy needle was inserted and a sample taken. My whole body was shaking uncontrollably. The nurse who was present asked in a kindly voice if I had anyone with me. "No" I replied in a raspy, almost inaudible voice, "I didn't think that I would need anyone." I hadn't expected that I would require support. I simply didn't expect this to happen.

The biopsy sample was taken away to be tested by another expert in a white coat. For some reason, he was introduced to me, but my brain was not receptive to remembering his name. I was in survival mode, feeling the *fight or flight* hormones rush throughout my body. Unfortunately, I could neither fight nor flee, so I just lay pathetically on the bed my eyes focussing on nothing in particular.

Please let him have enough cells to test; I silently prayed to whoever was listening. At that moment, I was preparing myself to refuse a further biopsy. Neither my body nor my mind could cope with the trauma of another painful attack.

Good news of sorts came back shortly after. The expert who had tested the cells announced that the biopsy had gathered enough to provide an accurate diagnosis. *Thank you,* I thanked whoever had listened to my prayer.

I was in a daze, hugging the gown to my body, as I crawled off the bed. Walking with feet like lead, I headed through the door and towards a changing room to put my clothes back on. Passing, I glanced at the serious faces of the few women waiting outside the ultrasound room. *Oh dear,* I realised that they'd heard me screaming! That was probably the last thing they wanted, particularly as they may be about to suffer the same fate.

In the changing room, I dressed on autopilot and returned upstairs to see the consultant again. The difference in atmosphere in the consultant's office was palpable. The cheerful demeanour had gone, replaced by a kindly but serious demeanour. This time there weren't any jokes or smiling. Feeling the knot in my stomach tighten, as I waited for him to speak, I wasn't surprised when he explained that something extremely suspicious had been detected by the mammogram.

I enquired in an urgent tone, "Is it definitely cancer?" I needed to know, and know then. I couldn't wait for the test results to come back. He took off his glasses, and his eyes met mine, as he replied, "It probably is cancer." However, he wouldn't say categorically as he had to wait until the results came back.

I don't remember the drive home. It felt as if I had left a part of my consciousness in the hospital when the biopsy had been taken.

I was due to return for confirmation of my test results a week later, and the consultant had advised me to take someone with me on that occasion. I knew I had to tell John as soon as possible. I felt physically sick as I thought about what I was going to say; words going around in my head, somehow not sounding quite right.

That evening during dinner, I nonchalantly suggested to John, that we go to the pub for a drink afterwards. Fighting to keep myself calm, I chatted with my husband in a casual tone which disguised the inner torment I was feeling. I knew he, like me, always saw going to the pub for an hour or so as a nice treat to be able to talk, just the two of us. This would make it almost impossible to utter the words *I probably have breast cancer*. However, I couldn't tell him at home, in case either of the girls overheard our conversation.

As we drove closer to the pub we often frequented, my stomach was churning so loudly I was sure John could hear it. Parking in one of the few spaces left in the busy car park and walking to the pub seemed almost surreal. I was feeling as if I was a stranger in my body, which was going through the motions without much direction from myself.

Ironically the scenario vaguely reminded me of the time I announced that I was pregnant. A different pub, in another town. On that occasion, I was nervous but happy; this time there seemed no real upside to what I was going to say.

Sitting down at the bar was not ideal for what I was about to say, but all the tables were taken. It was the only option available and preferable to standing around waiting, perhaps in vain, for someone to vacate a table.

The knot in my stomach felt as if it had taken a life of its own and was drawing tighter by the second. My palms were tacky with perspiration, and I could feel my adrenal glands pumping out adrenalin and cortisol as my body launched itself once again into the fight or flight stress response. Unable to run away, I had to focus on forming the words that my throat seemed too dry to utter. After taking a slow sip of my soda water and lime, I glanced at John's contented smile. *How can I shatter this moment of joy?* My thoughts were screaming in my head, *Just go for it!*

After a couple of deep breaths, I launched into one of the hardest conversations of my life so far, and simply said, "I went to the hospital today," and without waiting for John to show his surprise at that comment, I ploughed on by dropping the bombshell, "I probably have breast cancer."

John just stared at me, wide-eyed, with shock written on his face. After a moment or two of stunned silence, which seemed to last for hours, John found his voice and started to ask me for more details about what had happened. We then discussed my appointment in depth, down to the tests and comments made by the consultant.

In line with my thinking at that time, we decided not to let anyone else know until after I was given confirmation of my results the following week. Although I knew in my heart what the outcome would be, it seemed better to tell people when we knew exactly what the diagnosis was and what the proposed treatment options were. I was still in a numb state of shock. However, it was good to be able to have shared my situation with John, after all, we had shared a lot during the years we had been together.

Chapter 2

Finding Hope Deep Within My Being

Hope is always there even in the darkest of places; we just need to look.

The waiting was difficult to endure, and a week seemed like an eternity. My thoughts often returned to the same question, *Why does it take so long to get a diagnosis?* And the statement, *Perhaps I should have gone to the other hospital.* Although logic told me that it probably wouldn't have made any difference.

I wanted to take positive action, not sit around moping and worrying. I knew that sitting around doing nothing but tormenting myself with negative talk would not change the outcome; it would simply make me feel worse.

What am I going to do to keep my mind off what is happening to me? I then remembered the Harry

Edwards Spiritual Healing Centre.

My sister had told me about this healing centre many years previously. I had discovered a year or so before that it was located only a few miles from where I lived. My subconscious seemed to be telling me; *a spiritual healing session could be just what I need to help me calm down and come to terms with my situation.*

I was prepared to do almost anything to help myself relax and de-stress, if nothing else. Once I had decided that some spiritual healing was what I needed, I immediately looked up the phone number for the Harry Edwards Centre on the internet. I felt truly blessed, when I telephoned, as due to a cancellation, they could book me in for a healing session the very next day.

The Centre is situated within a picturesque 18th Century mansion house set in an idyllic backdrop. Driving up towards the mansion surrounded by stunning old oak trees, I was already feeling slightly less tense. During my short walk from the car park to the house, I caught sight of the well-tended gardens which flag the magnificent building. Pushing open the creaky old wooden door, I entered an impressive hallway with a solid wood reception desk located to my right. The friendly, efficient receptionist acknowledged that they were expecting me. Gesturing to a small room filled with comfortable chairs, she asked me if I would please wait a few minutes until called. My reception was so welcoming and friendly; I could feel my trepidation slowly disintegrating.

The waiting room was immediately off the hallway next to an impressive staircase. The décor inside engendered a feeling of calm, with soft music playing and comfortable furnishings. Looking out the tall sash window I could see more of the beautiful formal gardens. Immaculate lawn bordered by colourful flower beds. I pondered how different it was from the sterile, stark atmosphere in the hospital waiting room. Yes, I could already feel myself beginning to relax. After only a few minutes, a friendly, homely, older woman entered the room and asked me to follow her to the treatment room. We walked through the carpeted hallway, down a few stairs and through to where the treatment rooms were. Chatting about the weather to pass the time. Smiling, I commented on how stunning the surroundings were.

The treatment room itself was everything I could have hoped for, when in need of some spiritual healing. The soft music added to the ambiance of the pastel coloured room, which also looked out onto the formal gardens of the stunning mansion. Surrounded by the beautiful mature woodland and gardens, I was feeling the essence of true love located in this place. Before commencing the healing, I was asked some questions as I sat in a comfortable chair by the window.

I briefly explained the mental anguish I was going through, whilst exploring the kindly eyes of the lady healer. She seemed to understand my situation. Handing me a tissue when I broke down in tears, as I explained my dilemma. I just didn't know how to tell my two precious daughters about what was happening. I was so worried about how the news would impact upon them.

I cried until, with sore, puffy eyes, my gentle sobs subsided. Giving me time to compose myself, she then ushered me to the healing couch and made sure I was comfortable with a blanket over me, whilst adjusting the volume of the music so that it was not too loud for me.

As I lay back, my body seemed to melt into the warm, restful couch. Closing my, dry, gritty eyes, I knew this would be just what I was craving. Solace from the reality of my situation. To begin with, the session was so comforting and peaceful, feeling the warmth from the healer's hands gently touching my shoulders. Then without warning, waves of intense emotion surged through me. Tears rolled from my eyes, which moments before were dry as if there were no more tears left. Then, just as quickly these intense sensations subsided, into a feeling of complete calm. From somewhere deep inside my being, despite my current emotional state, I had the feeling that *everything is going to be okay!* This feeling for me encompasses the sheer magic of spiritual healing.

The lady healer who had been treating me was so kind and understanding of my situation. Afterwards, she then told me about the Bluebell's Cancer Support group run at the Centre, which coincidentally was running on that day. "Would you like me to introduce you?" she enquired in a kindly tone. "Yes," I replied in a croaky voice, barely a whisper. It seemed, somehow, as if it was perfect timing, it was simply *meant to be*. Following behind the kindly healer, I tentatively walked into the room, not knowing what to expect. I was introduced to a group of lovely smiling ladies who were sitting around a large square coffee table drinking tea and eating biscuits. Inviting me to join them, they gave me the airtime to talk about how I felt.

I can see their faces to this day, although, I cannot remember any of their names. I was in a trance-like state of shock and grief. Telling them my story seemed to catapult me into feeling like a stranger in my own body. I had a desire to somehow will myself to step back out of the nightmare and go back to just being me. The *me* I had been before; without this stomach gripping fear encroaching on my being.

I talked about my expected diagnosis and could feel the tears welling up again. *Tears are good,* I heard a small voice inside reassure me. The talking and the crying helped me that day, and I am forever grateful to those women for giving me the space to voice my fears without question. Going around the table, in turn, the others briefly shared some of their stories. I no longer felt quite so alone. However, simultaneously, I was experiencing a growing feeling of concern for what I was about to face.

Within the assurances of the others, was a shared experience of having no control over the situation they were in and somehow being at the behest of the doctors, the experts. Having no say in what was being done to their bodies. With a growing feeling of unease and doom, I listened to the stories behind the smiles of those lovely, beautiful creatures. The explanations of things not quite working out how they had hoped. The gut-wrenching stories from most of those in attendance who had experienced cancer recurring, after their initial treatment. And of how they were continuing to fight on despite the odds being increasingly stacked against them.

Shrouded in optimistic tones, the undercurrent of fear was palpable. I went into blocking mode to zone out the feeling of doom which was slowly creeping up on me. Concentrating hard on not allowing the negativity of my thoughts to consume me, a question cutting into my conscious mind, *there has to be another way?*

To finish the session, there was a hands-on healing session. Afterwards, as we said our goodbyes, I agreed to go back the following week and let all those kindly souls know how my next appointment at the hospital turned out. I left the Harry Edwards Centre that day with a bag of mixed feelings and thoughts, overplayed by a feeling of complete calm which I hadn't experienced in a long time.

It is true to say that I drove home with more questions about what was happening to my body than answers about what I could do. However, somewhere in the depth of my being was the faintest glimmer of hope. I wanted to cherish this stirring of hope from deep within, and nourish it. *But how,* I reasoned, *do I keep positive and in control?*

Day-to-day I was attempting to keep doing things in as normal a fashion as possible, for my own sanity and for the sake of the family. This was often difficult as *normal* is not a word I would have used at the time to describe how I felt. If anything, I felt abnormal, I had a tumour growing inside me that was probably cancerous. *That's definitely not normal,* I wanted to exclaim out loud. But I kept silent, swallowing down my screams.

On the Saturday after my first hospital appointment, I was running a Reiki training course at a local health clinic, where I occasionally ran my courses. I didn't want to start cancelling the commitments I had in my diary. I also had a vague sense that somehow things might not be so bad. I relished these thoughts; the *glass is half full* optimism helping to keep me centred. Enabling me to continue with my life as much as possible.

As I was clearing up the teacups in the kitchen, after the course was finished, I happened to notice a book entitled 'Cancer is not a Disease It's a Survival Mechanism' by Andreas Moritz. Surprised and intrigued, I simply had to find out what the author meant by his non-orthodox title. Opening the pages tentatively, I read a few random paragraphs. 'Wow,' my mind was suddenly fully alert. It seemed contrary to everything I had been told about cancer.

Moritz was challenging the very core of what is generally believed about cancer. He claimed that 'a person who is afflicted by the main causes of cancer (which constitute the real illness) would most likely die quickly unless he actually grew cancer cells,' and 'cancer will only occur if the body's main healing defense mechanisms have already failed.'[2]

Moritz even went further by stating that, 'To treat cancer as if it were an illness without removing its underlying cause is nothing but malpractice,' and furthermore, 'Instead of reducing cancer occurrence and cancer mortality, the current medical approaches used to treat cancer actually contributed to increasing both.'[3] I could feel a shiver of excitement going up my spine accompanied by goosebumps. This seemed such a radical idea, but nevertheless plausible. Then a sense of hope engulfed me like a warm blanket, giving me comfort as I packed my Reiki couch and training materials away. *What if this is true?* I pondered, *does this perhaps give me other options?*

On my drive home from the clinic, Moritz' book was still in my mind. *I hope I can purchase a copy of the book online,* I deliberated. Smiling as I shifted my black Ford Focus up into fifth gear with a new-found determination.

After dinner that evening, with growing excitement, I logged onto my desktop computer located in the corner of the dining room. Finding Moritz's book easily on Amazon, I purchased it without delay. Delivery was scheduled for the following week. Excited by what I might discover, I couldn't wait for it to arrive. I was eager to learn more of what this author had to say.

The following Tuesday, I found myself once again at the hospital; with John sitting next to me this time, giving me his unquestioning support. We were sitting uncomfortably in the badly designed plastic chairs provided for hospital outpatients. As I waited there, I could feel the trepidation growing within me. My mind felt as if it was filled with a strange fog which was affecting my thought processes. What didn't help was having to wait over an hour without being called. I wanted to scream out, 'I can't wait any longer!' At the same time, I didn't really want to be called and hear the expected prognosis.

I stood up and walked over to the rather harassed receptionist and enquired, "Can you please tell me why I'm having to wait such a long time?" Looking up from her computer keyboard, she announced in an exasperated tone, "Your notes have not yet arrived from downstairs."

I was becoming irrational in my thoughts. *It feels like a conspiracy,* I deliberated internally, *adding even more stress to me when I am already feeling at the end of my tether.* I could feel anger rising from the pit of my stomach, as I marched back to over to where I had been sitting. I exclaimed acerbically to John, "They have only had a week to get my notes here!"

I knew I was being illogical. However, I had to let my feelings out somehow, and it didn't seem appropriate to vent my anger on the receptionist.

The hard, plastic chair was becoming more uncomfortable, no matter which way I sat. The words on the magazine I was attempting to read appeared to be swimming in front of my eyes. *Hold it together,* I admonished myself. Closing my eyes gently, I proceeded to take a few deep breaths, to help me calm down.

Eventually, I heard my name, "Rhona Byrne." I was the last patient in the waiting room to be seen. *Is this an omen?* My irrational mind kicked in again. Taking another deep breath, I stood up on legs which seemed to want to stay rooted to the spot. Linking John's left arm, he led me to the consulting room.

I knew in my heart that the news would not be good. I was expecting the worst, as John and I sat down next to the consultant and nurse in the confines of the windowless room. The consultant proceeded to explain that indeed I did have breast cancer, which was oestrogen positive. However, "We have caught it early" he continued. I was advised that what I needed was to have an operation to remove the lump, followed by some radiotherapy to ensure that all cancerous cells are removed. My thoughts were racing, *He makes it all sound so routine. I guess it is for him. It's not routine for me!* I wanted to yell.

Meanwhile, the consultant was explaining that their expert panel of cancer specialists had decided that I should have an MRI scan. As they were unsure of the size of the tumour, and whether it had spread, the MRI results would provide them with further detail for a more accurate diagnosis.

"I am claustrophobic," I explained in a squeaky, childlike voice, "can my husband come in with me." *I sound so feeble*, I thought. Acutely aware of my vulnerability.

"Well it is up to you whether you have the scan or not" replied the consultant, "However, you will have to go in alone. I can operate without it, but this may mean that we find something unexpected during the operation." *Why am I feeling so helpless?* my mind was questioning. Resigning to his expertise, "Okay then, I guess I will try." I felt like a pawn - small and insignificant; powerless, almost without a voice. *My destiny is going to be in this consultant's hands;* the realisation struck me like a slap across the face, *I am compelled to do what he tells me, despite what I believe.* This thought left me numb with shock and fear.

We were told that it would take a few days for the

MRI scan to be booked. I would then have to wait again until there was another appointment available to see the consultant to receive my results. *Oh, my god, this is not a quick process!* I realised. Thinking about the delays, I was encountering, as I waited to receive a full diagnosis; *meanwhile, the cancer is inside me – growing!* My thoughts then returned to my two daughters. *How can I tell them that their mum has cancer?* It is not something you want to tell your children, especially when they are only twelve and fourteen.

The kindly, caring nurse then escorted us both into another room. She handed me a folder with all sorts of information on breast cancer. This was aimed at helping us understand the various procedures I would undergo. She continued by explaining to us what would happen, in soft reassuring tones. My thoughts, which were awash with confusion, gained focus with a random notion, *I am so glad I don't have her job!* I didn't say much at this stage, as my throat felt constricted and even breathing was a challenge. When we walked out of the room, I could hardly remember what the nurse had said. I was just aware that I would now have to wait even longer before anything was done!

On the way home in the car, John and I discussed how it might not be as bad as we thought because they had *caught the cancer early* and hopefully everything would be okay. However, something was troubling me. *How do they know if they have caught it early if they don't know what size it is and they need to do further tests?* I declined to share my ruminations with John. I didn't feel that it would be helpful to share anything negative with him at this stage.

Upon our arrival back home, John decided to fetch a takeaway, whilst I stayed home to tell the girls. Neither of us felt like cooking dinner after what we had been through, and I knew that it was time to reveal my diagnosis to Caitlin and Melissa.

My heart felt as if it was breaking when I explained my situation to them. "No!" they cried out in unison. Looking at their sad teary eyes, I worried silently about the effect the next few months would have on them. We hugged, they sobbed, and I sobbed, I felt sick, thinking *how can I do this to my girls, they are so young?* When John came home, he and I both attempted to explain that we had *caught the cancer early*, and everything was going to be okay. Although I had doubts and didn't really believe this, I kept this opinion to myself.

I had been planning to go out that evening. Despite feelings of guilt at leaving my loved ones, I really felt that it was a good thing. I needed to go out and talk to someone else. *Am I being unfair going out?* I debated with myself. However, dealing with such strong emotions from some of the people you love most in the world isn't easy to take. I reasoned *I am already committed to catching up with the others in my spiritual group.* We met once a fortnight in the local pub. I was the organiser, which made my decision easier.

As we sat in the pub, I was feeling a sense of calm after the storm. Compared to the earlier trauma, it was so much easier telling my spiritual friends. The discussion was more practical, and my deep emotions were given a rest for a while. Louise, who runs the clinic where I had been doing my Reiki course the previous week, came along to this meeting. She spoke about how her mother had recently *lost her battle* with breast cancer.

Louise explained how she had tried to help her mother by suggesting a variety of different alternative therapies. I could see the pain in Louise's eyes as she explained the tragic story of how her mother, to whom she was very close, eventually died. In our discussion, I also asked her about the Andreas Moritz book, which I had seen at the clinic. She explained that it is worth reading as it deals with cancer in a non-conventional way. I was certainly intrigued and was glad I already had it on order.

Gerry, another member of the group, who was at the meeting that evening, had been diagnosed with bladder cancer the previous year. Although he had had an operation to remove his tumour, he had refused any chemotherapy or radiotherapy. I was curious. He told me briefly about some of the alternative healing methods he had been employing. These therapies appeared to be helping him. This discussion with Gerry planted some more ideas in my head.

There it was again - the faintest glimmer of *Hope*. This time I felt it just that bit stronger, and it lasted a fraction of a second longer. YES, it was 'Hope' with a capital 'H'! *I am a Reiki healer, after all, perhaps there is more I can do to help myself?* I experienced a strange sense of liberation, if only for a few moments. These positive sensations led me to the conclusion that, *I must investigate alternative therapies in more detail, to see what I can do for myself.*

Besides the spiritual healing, I had received at the Harry Edwards Centre, my friend Alison sent me some distant healing. As I lay in my bed that night, I could feel a presence beside me bringing an energy into my body, which I experienced as a soothing, calming, healing energy. It is difficult to explain in words the sensations I experienced, as my body received the healing; leaving me feeling that *everything will be okay.*

To someone who has never received an in-person or distant healing session, it is difficult to explain how potent it can feel. A few days later, my friend Alison then came to visit me. During that visit, she kindly treated me to a Shamanic Healing session. What

I experienced during that session was extremely powerful and again difficult to put into words. The experience left me with a feeling of happiness and total calm.

I had never tried Shamanic Healing before. Most of the healing sessions I had previously experienced involved Reiki, as that is what I had specialised in. However, I can certainly say that Alison's healing session that day, touched me on a very deep level. It seemed that it was on this level that much of the healing was needed. This, I now know, was helping to take me deep into my subconscious, opening me up to where I had unexplored issues that I needed to work on. This is where many of my deep routed problems lay.

There were times when I wondered about what had happened to me, despite my knowledge and experience of healing, good nutrition, and exercise. I was acutely aware of the importance of these in relation to wellbeing. At one stage, my frustration took over, and I remonstrated with myself, *You have been teaching this wellness stuff for years!* Then, just as quickly, I realised that what I had been doing up until this point was simply good, but it was just not good enough. Yes, I knew the theory of what it takes to be healthy and happy, but somewhere I had become stuck on my path to wellness, and the cancer was the result.

What I need to do, is be kind to myself, I realised with a faint smile playing on my lips. This is what I had been teaching others these past few years. There it was again, that feeling of 'Hope' where many would think I should be in despair. Wayne Dyer refers to this in his book 'There is a Spiritual Solution to Every Problem'. He explains, 'What is hope but a feeling of optimism, a thought that says things will improve, it won't always be bleak, there's a way to rise above the present circumstances,' when referring to the well-known quote from the prayer of Saint Francis of Assisi. [4] When Saint Francis beseeches 'Lord, make me an instrument of thy peace', and in line five of the prayer 'Where there is despair *(let me sow)* hope'.

As agreed, John and I did not tell too many people about my diagnosis, at this stage. We decided to wait at least until we had the results from the MRI scan. My sister, Carolyne, was one person I was aware I could confide in. As we don't have any other siblings, she and I have a special bond. Despite the physical distance between us, we communicate regularly. Carolyne lives in Sydney, Australia, which made it difficult to tell her on the telephone about what I was going through. I would have preferred to be able to chat about my emotions with her face to face.

Carolyne called me shortly after I messaged her to say that I needed to talk to her. We chatted on the phone for a long time. It was an emotional conversation; she explained how she wished she could be with me to help me through my ordeal. We both knew, practically at that time, it was not possible. As a Reiki Master and spiritual healer herself, Carolyne promised to send me some distant healing. Our chat raised my spirits because there is no one else in the world who understands me as well as she does.

We both know that there is a strong connection between us, which can only be described as spiritual in nature. People often comment on how attached we are to each other. When we chat on the phone, the distance in miles between us seems to evaporate.

In January 2015, I had been lucky enough to travel out to Australia to spend a month with her. This was a special time for us both. With what was happening to me now, I was so glad that I had taken that opportunity to spend this exclusive period with her. Our time together, during those four precious weeks, will remain vivid in my memory forever. It seemed as if it was meant to be.

We also told John's mother, Philomena (Philo for short), who relayed the message to the rest of his family, most of whom live in Ireland. Their initial reaction was shock, followed by loving words of kindness and support, with a promise of prayers especially from Philo, to help me. It comforted me tremendously to know that others were sending me loving thoughts and praying for me.

The day after we telephoned Philo, John's sister, Yvonne sent me an inspirational YouTube Link. I watched the speaker, Anita Moorjani, in amazement as she relayed her moving story, of how she had completely recovered from multiple cancers, after a near-death experience. Almost unbelievably, Anita, who was only given hours to live, as her organs were shutting down, had regained consciousness. She then brought herself back from the brink of death, and despite suffering from 'incurable' cancer, had healed her body totally with love.

I watched Anita's video, with the fascination and excitement of a child who sees snow for the first time. Another glimmer of something I was now beginning to recognise, ran through me making me shiver. Yes, it was 'Hope' again, and the belief that there was a power far greater than that of a man or woman. There was an understanding emanating from deep within me, that faith, belief, and love, play such a vital role in our wellbeing. Going beyond thought, it was that 'knowing' being released from deep within my subconscious. At this stage, I wasn't at all aware of the importance of what I was experiencing. However, it did help me to focus on something other the misery of my current situation.

Bringing my awareness back to the questions raised by Andreas Moritz, on whether more could be done for cancer sufferers than simply 'cutting and burning' to 'cure' them. In his words, 'neither surgery nor the other two main treatment procedures (chemotherapy and radiation) remove the cause(s) of cancer.'[5] The assumption being, that if the cause is not removed, then there is a strong possibility that the cancer will return.

Questioning myself now, *what caused my breast cancer?* Answering this question was, I now realised, crucial to my healing. Interestingly, this is something that was ignored by the health professionals I had seen. *Why?* Another query that came to mind, with the only response I could fathom at the time, *because, for whatever reason, the specialist doctors are not trained to do that!*

I understood that even though the official statistics appeared to indicate that survival rates from breast cancer were good, this was not always the case. We all know of people who didn't survive, despite all the treatments offered by the medical profession. One of those, my mother's sister, who had died before I was born, had been diagnosed with breast cancer. Although medical treatment should have moved on significantly since then, I was not convinced.

Predominant in my mind when I remember discussing

her untimely death is my mother explaining to me, "Lena died a horrible death from the side effects of the treatment!" This statement, which has been forever etched in my memory, highlighting my mother's pain at having to stand by helplessly and watch the deterioration in her own sister's health. Being unable to do anything to prevent Lena's painful death at the young age of forty-five.

During my teenage years, another aunt of mine had died of leukaemia, and I had witnessed her demise, as she suffered the excruciating side effects of harsh chemotherapy drugs. Changing her from a bubbly, happy, caring person into an emaciated, sad, pain riddled shadow of her former self. I kept coming back to the reasoning *there has to be another way?*

Only two years prior to my diagnosis, John's father, Charlie, had died at the young age of sixty-two. Charlie had been diagnosed with cancer of the oesophagus and had also suffered immensely from complications brought on by the chemotherapy treatment he had to endure. The side effects of medical treatment which he had been prescribed eventually became too much for his body to withstand, dying a painful and untimely death, as the family stood by helplessly grieving their loss. Yes, I had witnessed the pain of cancer including the powerlessness felt by friends and family as they watch their loved ones deteriorate, before their eyes, resulting from the side effects of the prescribed *cure.*

Somehow, I was beginning to believe, without having full knowledge or understanding why, that there must be another way. I recognised that conventional medicine, although it can appear to work wonders, was not so successful in when it came to cancer treatments. In fact, existing treatments for cancer patients, which I had observed first hand, seemed to me to be barbaric and cruel.

What started as the merest glimmer of 'Hope' that I could find another way to heal my body, was now growing into an undeniable surge, pulsating through my body trying desperately to eliminate the gripping fear that accompanies a diagnosis of cancer.

Chapter 3

The Road Less Travelled

It is not easy to go where others are afraid to tread.

Early on Saturday morning on 19th September 2015, John drove me to the hospital where I was to have my MRI scan. Ironically, after my reservations, I had been given an appointment within a short time frame, and so there I was sitting in yet another waiting room. Ironically, even though it was in an NHS hospital, this one was more comfortable than the others.

The MRI department is run by a private company, and the surroundings reflected that. The chairs were more comfortable, and there was even a machine which dispensed free tea, coffee, and hot chocolate. The young, friendly receptionist seemed eager to put me at ease. Handing me a form she kindly asked me to complete it. I enquired if John could come into the room whilst I was having the scan. "Yes, of course" she exclaimed, to my delight. Then explained that he would have to complete a form to ensure that there was no reason that would prevent him being with me, such as a pacemaker or any metal lodged within his body. With the formalities over, all we had to do was wait. As the MRI unit had just opened for the day, there was no one else waiting. We sat down together next to a low coffee table with some neatly stacked magazines on it. Flicking absentmindedly through one of the magazines, I couldn't bring myself to read anything. Despite the comfortable surroundings, I could feel my body trembling and struggled to steady my hands as I held the superfluous magazine.

I was then led into a waiting area near to the room within which the MRI scanner was located. The friendly male nurse explained that I would have some dye injected into my left arm prior to the scan. This was to highlight the tumour during the procedure so that it could be measured. I was just going through the motions again. Although I was dreading the procedure I was about to undergo; I was working hard on staying present and trying not to worry. Taking a few deep calming breaths, I allowed myself to relax as much as I could.

Simply taking each moment as it came, calmly and mindfully. I changed into a gown in one of the dedicated changing rooms and let myself be led through to where the MRI scanner was. Holding my right hand, John walked slowly by my side whispering to me in soft, soothing tones "I am here with you, and everything will be okay." He continued to talk to me as I lay face down on the part of the scanner which then retracted into the frame of the machine. I could feel my arms brushing against the inner wall of the machine as the bed I was lying on moved slowly inwards.

And breathe, I kept telling myself. As the clanking, banging, buzzing and clicking went on for what seemed like an eternity, I could feel John's hand gently touching my right foot. This was the only part of me he could reach as my whole body was inside the scanner. It was good to focus on something other than what I was going through. Keeping my thoughts on my feet was helping me to keep sane. I was so grateful to John for being there with me. In those moments, I felt truly loved. I know his presence helped me to endure what, for someone who doesn't even like travelling in lifts, was an enormous ordeal.

I can't remember much afterwards, apart from sitting in the passenger seat of John's SAAB looking out at the passing traffic with the clanking, banging, buzzing and clicking still resonating in my head. I remember breaking the silence between us by joking about the dye, "Now I know what it feels like to have blue blood." Somehow, the witty comment seemed to fall flat, and the silence resumed. We both knew that all we could do now was wait.

I believe there is another way to deal with my cancer.

This was not a conscious thought; it came from a deep inner knowing, which was growing within me day-by-day. This knowing resulted in a plethora of emotions, including joy, optimism, hopefulness, and even happiness. Many people may find this almost impossible to understand. Even within my own family, my husband John did not comprehend the way I viewed my condition.

"How can you be so positive about everything that is happening to you?" he often commented.

My instinct was crying out to me; *I know I can deal with my cancer in a non-conventional and loving way.* I simply did not want to *fight* as most people do. I wanted to be in control of my own destiny, without the intervention medical professionals, no matter how well meaning they were.

Lying awake in bed, in the still depth of the night, I instinctively sent my tumour love. Saying a silent *thank you* to my cancer for giving me the opportunity to change my life. Changes I had yet to fathom. Taking inspiration from others, including Andres Moritz, when he states, 'the most common cause of ill' *health* is, 'not loving yourself.' [6] And turning this around to loving myself to improve my health. Not only had I been teaching this in my seminars and workshops, I really believed that it was true. Now, it seemed that I had been given the opportunity put it into practise. It was undeniably an enormous challenge for me to tackle.

I resolved that the fewer people I told this to, the

easier it would be for me to cope. I figured that all the emotional energy I would use trying to explain the inexplicable would be a drain on my valuable resources. I needed all the energy I had to work on a way forward to deal with my current situation.

One week exactly after my diagnosis, John and I returned once again to the hospital to receive the results of my MRI scan. I was holding onto my newly found optimism which imbued serious doubts in my mind about the options (or lack of them to be precise) the medical profession offers people who have cancer. It seemed that the 'cut and burn' option had no alternatives.

As John and I endured this meeting with the consultant, I simply sat in silence. There was nothing to say. The details of what would be done to me were explained in a manner that left no room for question. John had fully expected to see the results of the MRI scan in full detail on the consultant's computer screen, so that we could come to realise first-hand the extent of the tumour growth. What in fact we received, was a rough hand drawn sketch which the consultant proceeded to create as we sat there. It depicted an odd looking female character with two round boobs, one of which had a mark on it to represent the tumour. What incensed John most at the time was the smile on the face of this roughly sketched cartoon character.

The consultant explained that I had invasive oestrogen positive breast cancer, which may have spread to my sentinel lymph nodes. *Oh, my God!* I found it hard to breathe. I felt as if some unseen object was constricting to flow of air into my lungs, and swallowed hard to clear the lump in my throat. The full diagnosis sounded really scary!

When John asked what "stage" the cancer was, the consultant simply sidestepped the question by saying that the stage was unimportant. This seemed a bit peculiar, but I wasn't in the right frame of mind to question it.

I was focussed so deep within my own distressing thoughts; *I can't let him inject me with radioactive dye and butcher me,* that I didn't even notice it. Later when John and I discussed the sketch, we concluded that it was extremely unprofessional and not particularly helpful as well as degrading and hurtful.

During this meeting, I was also asked if I would participate in a trial regarding removal of my lymph nodes. Although the consultant tried to explain what was involved, I didn't really understand what the trial entailed, only that I would have to sign a permission slip prior to my operation. What I could ascertain was that tests would be done on the lymph nodes under my left arm.

Listening to the consultant, I was under the impression that what happened next would depend upon the results of those tests. Therefore, some or all of the lymph nodes under my left arm may have been removed during the same operation. What I discovered later, upon reading the paperwork I was given by the nurse after this meeting, was a completely different scenario. The plan was to remove some of my lymph nodes during the operation to test them and, not that they would simply be tested without removing them first.

In some ways, the outcome was the same. There

would be no further discussion with me about the need to remove some or all of my lymph nodes and the risks involved. Knowing how vital the lymph system is to our wellbeing, I was feeling extremely uncomfortable even thinking about it. I likened it to the detrimental result of removing a filter from the engine of a car, only much more devastating.

I had met women who have had serious repercussions including lymphoedema, after having had their lymph nodes removed. Lymphoedema is a chronic (long-term) condition which causes the arm and hand to swell up with fluid (which should have drained through the lymph system) which now, as a result of lymph removal, basically has nowhere else to go!

As the consultation ended, the walls of the small windowless room appeared to be closing in on me with claustrophobic effect. Ironically, I could feel the fear rise in my body in a way I had managed to avoid during my MRI scan. I was reacting to a sensation of helplessness, as if trapped by the circumstances. I felt railroaded into signing the permission slip for my operation.

My heart was screaming *NO!* but my head was saying, *What else can you do? You have no other choice but to sign.* Not having the strength to argue; I knew my pleas would fall on deaf ears. I wanted to get out of the consultant's office as fast as I could. Head pounding, I put pen to paper, imprinting an illegible scrawl, before the consultant ripped off a copy and presented it to me, for my records.

As John and I headed towards the exit, each one of our footsteps echoing on the polished laminate floors, I endured a dazed numbness. Gradually, the closer we were to 'escaping' from the antiseptic smell and clinical feel of the hospital corridors, I could sense a stirring of determination from deep within my core. An urge to do something positive and not conform to what I considered would be a *barbaric assault* on my body. The resulting outcome of which, would be under question, until I awoke afterwards.

I was certain that this was not what I wanted, even though I was unaware exactly what other options I had. I didn't know exactly how I would proceed. My desire, at that moment, was to do my own research and explore what I could do for myself.

A few days later, I started to read the information leaflet on the proposed trial which I had been given by the consultant. I discovered that more of what I thought the consultant had said was inaccurate. What was actually going to happen was: "Which treatment you get is decided by a process called randomisation. Neither you nor your doctor or nurse will be able to choose which group you are allocated to".

This means that I would have had partial, or complete removal of the lymph nodes under my left arm, not based on whether they needed to be removed, but simply to satisfy the statistics of the trial. Thus, I may have had all my lymph nodes removed without my consent, even if they were not affected by cancer! In some ways, in the short term, it would have been easier to just go along with and participated in this trial. If I hadn't read the information leaflet properly, or fully understood it, I might have just signed the consent form. Had other women done this because, like me, they were in a state of shock upon receiving their cancer diagnosis?

The information contained in the leaflet continued

to concern me: "In the event that something does go wrong and you are harmed during the study, there are no special compensation arrangements." This is with the proviso that: "We cannot promise the study will help you"! I felt that I was being swept up into a living nightmare. *Please, God help me out of this insanity,* I pleaded silently as the implications of what could happen to me hit me hard like a physical blow to my chest. I wanted to wake up and return to a world of sanity.

After this consultation, I was telephoned on a regular basis by those involved with the trial. They wanted me to confirm that I would take part. I just didn't want to think about it anymore and was far from making a decision. It got to the point that I was afraid to answer the telephone and simply left it to go to the answering machine. Although I can understand the need to do medical trials, I was sceptical about taking part in this one, as I was about the remainder of my proposed treatment.

In addition to my health concerns, there were many other things going on in my life at that time demanding my attention. One of these was my mother's health, as she had been in hospital for the previous three months. Now in her eighties, my mum had been in and out of hospital several times since the previous year, when she was given a pacemaker after collapsing at home during the night. This time she was suffering because she had broken her leg some months earlier, and was not recovering well.

My father was fretting about how he would manage to look after Mum when she came home, if she remained unable to walk. Also in his eighties, he had, up until that point in time, been upbeat and positive about how things were going with him being my mum's carer. His mindset was rapidly descending into one of constant worry about the future.

I desperately wanted to go to Scotland to see my parents. With that in mind, I took the decision to postpone the date of my surgery, so that I could travel to Scotland and visit them.

I experienced such a sense of relief when I called the hospital to inform the breast cancer nurses that I could not make the allocated date for my operation. In addition to spending quality time with my parents, staying in Scotland for a week gave me valuable thinking time. Whilst I was there, I proceeded to take each day as it came. Not really focussing on the future. As the purpose of my trip was about my parents, I spent time with my mum every day in the hospital and with my dad in the evenings. I had decided not to tell either of them about my diagnosis, so as not to worry them. They had enough to deal with. My mother's recovery from her broken leg was much slower than expected. In fact, whilst she was in hospital she had a subsequent fall and had to have her leg reset. The prognosis for her being able to walk again was not good. Being in Scotland without John and the girls, meant that I also had time alone. Spending some of it meditating and the remainder just simply ruminating about what I really wanted to do.

One thing was bothering me - and it wasn't the cancer - it was the revised date for my operation which was looming. My mind was constantly bombarding me with the realisation that, *I need more time to decide what to do.*

Even at this early stage of my journey, my fear was

not the cancer, as others would believe. My gut-wrenching dread emanated from the cold, hard reality of the possible side effects of the operation itself. The realisation that I would be injected with radioactive dye prior to the surgery on the premise of highlighting the lump. *Radioactive die* my thoughts screamed, *but radioactivity causes cancer!* I was by now convinced that letting this happen to me felt fundamentally wrong.

It was if my whole being was crying out to me, *Don't let them do it.* I didn't think that I was being stupid, as logic was constantly bombarding me with the same thought: *Why would anyone want to inject a carcinogenic substance into someone who has cancer?* For me to have developed a tumour in the first place, I knew that my immune system needed to have been seriously compromised.

I wholeheartedly believed that the kind of treatment that the surgeon was proposing would only make me more unwell. During this time, I reached an unequivocal level of certainty that surgery plus radiotherapy and possibly chemotherapy, was not the way I wanted to go.

Upon my return home from Scotland, I resolved to *do my own thing* and work on my own self-healing. I postponed my surgery one more time. This time I explained that I simply didn't think my immune system was up to the operation. I was speaking my truth. I believed categorically that the cancerous tumour would not have grown in the first place if my immune system had been fully functional. However, I didn't elaborate by explaining my overriding concern that I didn't consider surgery to be a good idea at all. I was fully aware that I would soon have to face my next biggest fear – confronting the consultant and telling him that I was unwilling to accept his obligatory treatment. I could not keep postponing the operation indefinitely!

From somewhere deep inside me I was holding onto my *knowing* that I wanted to take control of my own destiny and do what I felt was right. By this time, I had read Andres Moritz book 'Cancer is not a Disease' from cover to cover, and could see the sense in much of what the author had written. It had given me ideas, but nowhere near enough information to implement them. I was hungry for the vital pieces of the puzzle which would act as a guide and enable me to successfully heal myself without medical intervention. Without focussing too much on the enormity of the task I faced, my resolve was growing stronger by the day.

What happened next was much more than a coincidence. My friend Debbie sent me a link to a free online video series called 'The Truth About Cancer' which was created by an American called Ty Bollinger. The series ran for nine consecutive days from 13th to 21st October, and each episode was at least two hours long. I was hooked on watching every episode.

Every evening, after dinner, without fail, there I was sitting expectantly, straight-backed, buttocks resting on the padded cushion of one of my Yew wood dining room chairs. With an additional cushion to support my lower back, in front of the desktop computer in my dining room, I sat engrossed in the content as the series unfolded. I wasn't going to miss it for anything. Much to the annoyance of my family, particularly John, who simply could not understand why I was "wasting my time listening to some idiot on the internet."

Undeterred, I was captivated and listened to it avidly every day. The more I learned, the more convinced I became that having the operation, followed by radiotherapy and possibly chemotherapy was not the route for me.

Day by day, as the series unfolded, Ty interviewed doctors who had adopted alternative therapies for cancer, and survivors who had used those therapies tailored to their individual needs. I was increasingly encouraged to research and discover what I could do for myself.

By this stage, the deep inner knowing which had been growing in me had manifested in the decision to continue to send love to my cancer, and see it as a blessing. Many people may consider this to be foolish. However, it resonated with me. Intuitively, I understood I was somehow honouring myself with this unorthodox approach. This was not a thought, it was a *state of being*, emanating from deep within my soul. I thank God for this tacit knowledge which convinced me that dealing with the cause of my tumour, is where true healing lies.

I was changing my mindset, away from the assumption that healing cancer was about fixing the problem by dealing with the symptoms. I was now convinced that I needed to focus my energies on seeking out and healing the root cause. The more I thought about it; I realised that this seemed logical to me. The emphasis was on the positive and not the negative as with what the consultant had prescribed.

Consistent positive action was what I knew I needed, to enable me to execute my new healing regime.

I tackled my challenge in a positive way, by drawing on the mindfulness teachings I had absorbed over the previous two years. This was territory I recognised, understood and felt comfortable with. Rather than focussing on the enormity of the task I was undertaking, I just did what I could, each day, on that day and for that day. My focus was not on the future days, weeks or months. I was simply focussing on each day at a time. Each minute, practising gratitude for having the opportunity to change my life in this way.

I then began to make changes to my diet. Cutting out substances and foodstuffs which I already knew were not good for me, such as sugar, bread, dairy products, and coffee. Some people may see this as hard work. I relished it as an exciting challenge. I was also still receiving distant healing from friends and family as well as treating myself to Reiki healing on a regular basis.

This was certainly the time to put all my learning to date, into practice. Encouraged by the fact that I was not starting from scratch, as I already knew a great deal about healthy living. I bought books specifically on alternative approaches to healing cancer, from which I learned more comprehensive details on what I could do to help me to heal my cancer. Interestingly, much of what I came across was not new to me. I had been aware of it. I asked myself often *how is it that I can know so much, but it takes cancer to convince me that these things are what I should be doing?* By re-reading books I already owned, I was beginning to turn my 'shelf help' into 'self-help,' with tangible actions I could execute to help myself!

About a month into my new regime, I learned that rebounding is particularly good for activating the lymph system to help the detoxification process. As the lymph system is the body's way of eliminating waste products from the bloodstream, keeping it moving is crucial to healing. I decided that it would be a good idea to invest in a trampette. I had been looking at second-hand ones on the internet, many of which appeared to be well used. In an effort to get me moving, literally, John then went out and bought a new one for me. What a lovely surprise. I couldn't wait to get it out of its box and start jumping! I tried different moves to inject some variety into what can be a bit of a monotonous process. I also discovered to my delight that singing whilst rebounding is such a positive, fun thing too. It certainly amused the rest of the family seeing me jumping on my mini trampoline, whilst singing out of tune!

My key focus was now on doing all I could to feel better, which did not happen overnight. In fact, I definitely felt worse before I began to see the light at the end of the tunnel. All I had was my inner knowing to remind me that what I was doing was right for my family as well as for me. Initially, my body was going through a major detoxification process. I felt exhausted most of the time, and my body was amongst other things, omitting an unpleasant odour. I didn't want to be sicker than I had been, however, I felt that this was something I had to experience. I simply had to rid my system of the multitude of toxins which my body had been exposed to over the years.

I had previously considered myself to be reasonably fit, as I swam four to five times per week and attended a yoga class once a week. Unfortunately, I had been forced to give up playing tennis the year before due to a problem with my Achilles tendon. This had led me to swim more often, which I really enjoyed. At the time, I had not considered the consequences of exposing myself to a barrage of toxic chemicals from the swimming pool on such a regular basis. This meant that my depleted immune system was being bombarded by these chemicals every time I entered the swimming pool.

What I hadn't been doing was leaving myself much time to exercise outside. I did walk a few times a week to the local shops, however other than that I didn't get much fresh air. In addition to filling your lungs with much-needed oxygen, exercising outside helps to top up vitamin D levels. Much had been talked about recently, about the need for vitamin D and the link between deficiency and cancer.

Andreas Moritz covered this in his book 'Cancer is not a Disease', referring to numerous studies showing the importance of sunshine. In particular, the significance of Vitamin D in keeping us healthy. In addition, he explored the importance of sunshine to the secretion of serotonin by our bodies.[7] Serotonin is often referred to as the 'feel good' hormone.

Many of us work in offices and buildings with no natural daylight. It's no wonder that there is more and more sickness absence due to stress-related illness. If people were zoo animals, it would be deemed cruel to keep them in cages, sitting in one spot, staring at a computer screen for hours on end with no natural light. Add to that a diet of coffee and unhealthy snacks with lunch often eaten at the desk, and little or no exercise day after day! This is how many people live in our 'civilised' society. The real question here is, does this make people happy?

Only they know the answer to that question.

One of the many things that kept me going was my dog, Lenny. My life was transformed once he became a member of the family.

Lenny is a rescue dog, and we are unsure as to his full history. When we adopted him, the papers stated that he is part Lurcher. Light brindle in colour, he is too stocky to be only a Lurcher, and we think that he perhaps has some Staffordshire Bull Terrier in him too. However, his pedigree, or lack of it, was irrelevant to me. What was important was that he was always affectionate and fun loving.

Melissa and Caitlin had always wanted a dog. I was used to dogs, having always had them whilst growing up. Ever since I was five years old, when Rusty, our treasured golden retriever joined the family. Nevertheless, I'd been reluctant to have one as an adult.

I was focussed on the fact that looking after a dog could be hard work and a big responsibility. However, I had forgotten what joy they can bring. Lenny brought me lots of joy when I needed it most, particularly in the early days when my body was struggling to cope with the basic daily routine of showering, dressing, and eating.

I relished my walks with Lenny day after day. He seemed to spur me on when my exhausted body felt as if it would rather have gone back to bed. The exercise was good for me even when my fatigued body required me to stop frequently to catch my breath. Yes, Lenny helped my recovery in many ways. I always felt better after my walks with Lenny. Oxygenating my lungs and feeling it circulate throughout my body was vitally important. Exercising in nature was invigorating, and meeting people to pass the time of day all helped me physically, mentally and spiritually.

It seems ironic that I became much healthier after giving up my gym membership! Our hour-long walks every day around the lake near my home or through the woods at the local common; each day a new adventure with Lenny. Looking at the world through his eyes was a cathartic experience. Dogs are such good teachers, as they really show us how to live mindfully.

Lenny lives in the moment, with each day a new fresh adventure. Every moment an opportunity to sniff a fascinating smell or play chase with another dog, without a care in the world. They instinctively know how to have fun in the here and now. It always brings me such pleasure to watch Lenny play with other dogs. Running around in circles, chasing each other, play fighting - wonderful!

The combination of gentle exercise and fresh air was a key factor in my healing process. Even when I felt extremely ill during the initial days of my detoxification process, I always felt so much better after our walks. In those early days, I felt like my head was filled with cotton wool and my feet were like lead. I can't ever remember having experienced such exhaustion. Lenny helped me to live in the moment.

I discovered another benefit to spending time with Lenny was his ability to help me relax. He seemed to instinctively know that I was unwell. He would come and sit next to me on the sofa, as I lay down for my afternoon nap. The essential restorative sleep I so needed to help me recover. I would often meditate and then fall asleep afterwards, with Lenny's head resting on my lap. His soft brown knowing eyes looking at me as if he could see into my soul. He almost seemed to be willing me to get better!

Despite my positivity, I knew that I was going to have to tell John, the girls and worst of all the doctors that I intended to heal myself. I had to be honest about my intention to reject the planned operation and subsequent therapy. When first I announced my decision to John he was furious. He simply did not understand what I was doing, as he was, understandably, coming from a place of fear.

As mentioned previously, John's father had died of cancer of the oesophagus when he was only 62. John was consumed by the fear of losing me. In addition, as he explained later, he felt a sense of utter helplessness at being unable to do anything to change my situation.

He pleaded with me to at least have the operation, if not the suggested radiotherapy/chemotherapy. I stood my ground, with little evidence to prove my point. John had refused to look at all the material that I had been studying over the past few weeks. I persisted, and he shouted at me, "You must at least have the operation and let the doctor remove the tumour." Exhausted by the confrontation, I went to bed upset, whilst holding onto the knowledge that I was right, and I would hold on to this no matter what anyone else said.

I asked the angels for help. I knew that I was being guided by more than my own thoughts and beliefs. If that had been the case, I may have acquiesced and had the operation. My steely determination was being fed by my soul and a force far greater than myself.

What's in a song?

The next day as I was jumping on my mini trampoline, song kept going through my head. I found myself singing this song whilst jumping away:

Give me joy in my heart keep me praising
Give me joy in my heart I pray
Give me joy in my heart keep me praising
Keep me praising 'till the break of day.

As usual, my girls thought it was hilarious seeing mum jumping and singing when they came home from school. I felt so alive, so happy. This is mindfulness at its best simply being in, and enjoying the moment.

Whilst telling John later of the experience, he simply looked at me quizzically and announced, "that was my Grandmother, Nana Gaynor's favourite song." I thanked her silently for her support, *Thank you, Nana Gaynor, from the other side, for helping John to understand.* I could feel she was with me on my quest.

On 20 Friday, November 2016, I was once again sitting next to the consultant breast surgeon in his compact office. This time I was feeling strong and confident. When I announced that, after much thought, I had decided not to have the proposed operation.

He looked over his glasses stared straight into my eyes and warned, "Mrs. Byrne you are going to die."

Taking a deep, restorative breath I replied in a confident voice, "Thank you for your concern,

however, I have decided that it is just not right for me."
After a lengthy conversation, whereby the consultant
tried to persuade me to follow his treatment plan,
I managed to respectfully convince him that I was
resolute in my decision.

What I did request, however, was that I continue to be
monitored via ultrasound to check the tumour on a
regular basis. He kindly agreed to this, commenting
that I could change my mind at a later date if I wanted
to. I was sure I would not change my mind, however,
I thanked him for his concern, and went on my way.

In contrast to my previous visit with John, on
this occasion, I felt empowered upon leaving the
consultant's office. I was happy with the way I
had handled the consultation. I hadn't resorted to
arguing with the consultant that I was right. I had
simply stated firmly that I had made my decision, and
that was that. I said a silent thank you to the Angels
upon leaving the hospital that day. My journey back
to health had well and truly started!

Chapter 4

My Support Groups

When we ask the Universe for help, our friends appear.

Along with my seemingly never-ending research into alternative healing approaches, it was immensely beneficial to share my ideas with my spiritual and alternative therapy friends.

These people were already aware of my diagnosis, and as the weeks unfolded, I explained my radical concepts for rejecting conventional medicine in favour of doing my own thing. At that time, I wasn't sure exactly what that meant, however, it helped me to receive positive words of encouragement from those few spiritual friends in whom I had confided. That was the type of support I craved, as it enabled me to pursue my desire to help myself heal without invasive medical treatment.

I was uncertain how many of my other friends would react to my diagnosis. I was concerned that they would have seen me as sick and offered me sympathy. The last thing I wanted was for others to look at me as some helpless victim of a possibly life-limiting illness. I simply didn't want anyone to be thinking of me with negative, fear-based thoughts, no matter how well-meaning and caring they were.

This may seem to some people to be a harsh and selfish approach. To them, I will say, 'In life, we have to be true to ourselves,' and that is exactly how I perceived my situation. I was considering what I needed to serve me, whilst I faced the challenge I was experiencing. Yes, I now referred to my situation as a *challenge*, which in my mind could be perceived in a positive light. I was not a victim, and as such, I was determined to be in control of my own destiny.

Despite my resolve to do things my way, I am so grateful to the few friends who knew what I was doing, including those in my spiritual group, Starlight Spiritual - Surrey. I met with the group regularly and was able to confide in them and be honest about my feelings. Feelings that many people would simply not understand. My positive mindset was evident, as I eagerly discussed the next instalment in my healing journey. These rare individuals with whom I met on a regular basis, allowed me to discuss what I was planning to do. They understood, at least to some extent, what I was trying to do. A 'support group' of individuals who listened to what I had to say and supported me. What they didn't do was tell me I should have my tumour removed, or in any other way project any fear-based comments onto me. I am immensely grateful for their understanding and backing during the months that followed my diagnosis.

As I have explained, I did not confide in many people about my tumour, because I was not in need of their sympathy. I had people around me who didn't require me to justify what I was doing and why. This may sound irrational, as the idea of receiving sympathy when unwell can often be appealing. Those in my spiritual group did not display that they felt sorry for me in any way. This was the type of backing that I needed and wanted. My spiritual friends allowed me to describe what I was doing, without judgement.

We discussed my new regime, often in minute detail, with them giving me handy hints and tips to help me along the way. They helped to encourage me with their suggestions, which was what I desired more than anything else from others at that time.

The reason that I had originally set up my spiritual group, in June 2015, was primarily to become acquainted with more 'like-minded' people who were interested in spiritual topics. I could find no other similar groups in the local area, and my sister, Carolyne, had even suggested that I set up my own group. Some of those who joined and attended regular meetings and catch up sessions in the pub have become my friends. It is interesting that the Universe again delivered exactly what I needed when I needed it. These were people I could talk to, who didn't tell me to do what the doctors advised or advise me that having the operation would be the best option. They knew how passionately I believed what I was doing was right for me. They helped me to stand strong and resolute when I was working through my many healing options. I could sense that the Universe had delivered the support group I desired, just when I needed it most.

I also confided in some more of my other very close friends, including, Irene, who lives within driving distance, just north of London and the M25. After I divulged my story to her, she arranged to visit me within days of hearing my news. Irene and I have been friends since our college days, and it was lovely to pour my heart out to her in those early days; when I knew what I wanted but was still unsure how it was all going to manifest. She treated me to a lovely pub lunch, and we talked about old times. We laughed, and I cried, expressing some of the many emotions that had been building up in me over the preceding weeks; with my diagnosis, having to tell John and the girls what was happening, the hospital visits and the challenges with my mum's health. I needed to chat, and Irene's company was so comforting and enjoyable. I was feeling so blessed to have such a good friend.

Another of my friends, Morag, although initially wary of my unconventional decision, became accepting of my situation. After the initial shock of what I was going through she soon realised that I was going to do things my way and added her empathetic ear to my situation. She could understand my logic after I explained how I wanted to personally take control of my healing. As she lives in Scotland, it had been a few weeks before I was able to see her, but when I did, she expressed how my positive approach had inspired her.

Once I had explained in detail to John's mother, Philo and his brothers and sisters what I was doing, I could feel that in the main they were supportive of my decision. Although initially sceptical, my passion for what I was doing plus my resolve won them over.

To everyone who supported my decision to take an alternative healing journey, I say a massive 'thank you' from the bottom of my heart. Almost from the very start, I knew that sympathy was not what I required to facilitate my unorthodox regime.

I was aware that most people would simply not understand what I was doing, and may even try to persuade me to take the advice of the consultant and have conventional treatment. I wanted to avoid having to use up my valuable energy trying to justify my decisions to others. In fact, I wanted people who knew me to see me as fit and well, because I was working on the premise that I was essentially healthy. I was simply practicing what I preach. I believe wholeheartedly in the importance of positive energy through thought.

Chapter 5

Into The Never-Ending Recesses of My Subconscious

Faith, hope, and love - the essential trilogy.

I knew that my healing had to take place on all levels and not just physically. I also had to look at myself in both an emotional and spiritual way, and deal with any hurt or pain that I believe had contributed to the resulting tumour. I recognised that I had to go deep into the recesses of my being to discover the emotions that I needed to accept and release.

Having practised Reiki energy healing for several years, I was aware of both the positive and negative effects of energy. I had even been teaching in workshops how 'your biography becomes your biology,' explaining how positive thoughts and beliefs are vitally important to wellbeing. Although I had done a great deal of healing on myself over the previous seven years, I identified that somehow this wasn't enough. It was crucial to my healing regime that I did more, particularly on an emotional level; digging deep into my subconscious to discover what negative beliefs, thoughts, and feelings I was holding onto without having any knowledge of what these were or in fact of their very existence.

My friend Debbie, whom I met through my group Starlight Spiritual, introduced me to a healing therapy called Quantum Healing Hypnosis Technique (QHHT). This technique helped me to open the door to my subconscious being.

QHHT is a technique developed by hypnotist Dolores Cannon which involves inducing an individual into the somnambulistic state of trance through visualization. A state which, under ordinary circumstances, is usually only experienced twice daily. It is experienced during the moment just before you become consciously awake and the moment just before you fall asleep.[8] The technique aims to gain access via the subconscious mind, to significant experiences from the past, and past lives which have been lived by the individual, which are adversely affecting them. This is based on the belief that we can journey in time through our subconscious mind. A QHHT session, therefore, enables the recipient to find out what specifically from the past may be causing them problems in the here and now. Once the cause has been established, then instantaneous healings can be manifested when applicable.

I had previously attended a past life regression group session and had been unsuccessful in being able to visit any past lives. I decided, however, that it was worth a try. My reticence at how successful the session would be, disappeared after a discussion with Debbie. Her reassurances and kind nurturing nature put me instantly at ease and allayed my fears. I resolved, *If anyone could lead me in a regression session, Debbie would be the best person.*

I organised a Sunday morning session with her the following week. I was now keen to experience first-hand how a QHHT healing regression could benefit me. Debbie had explained that an initial session could last between two and a half to three hours. I couldn't quite fathom how this would happen, however, I placed myself in her expert hands. Before attending the session, Debbie had asked me to prepare a few questions on what specifically I would like answers and guidance. This was to enable her to conduct the hypnosis accordingly, to give maximum benefit to me. Before commencing we discussed a multitude of questions posed by Debbie, to ensure that she understood totally what I was seeking from the session.

I lay down on the soft, fluffy blanket covering her comfortable therapy couch; a feeling of calm began to come over me. I had never been hypnotised in a one-to-one situation such as this before, so I had been feeling slightly anxious before we started. Debbie's serene demeanour helped me to relax instantly. Her soothing voice put me at ease, as she proceeded to talk me into a hypnotic state. What was strange, is that I still seemed fully conscious of my surroundings throughout the whole session. It did take me a while to get any mental images, however, once it started the visions flowed easily. I went from one past life to another gathering information and healing as I went.

During the session, I discovered some of what happened to me in other lifetimes and how it was impacting upon me now. I went deep into these lifetimes, which was an intensely emotional experience. It involved re-experiencing some of what happened in those incarnations and how it related to my current situation. This enabled me to gain a greater understanding of my emotions and allowed me to send healing and forgiveness to myself and others involved.

Interestingly, I encountered many individuals with whom I have relationships with today, including my sister, my mother and my husband. The session, which lasted over three hours in total, was so powerful and cathartic. I felt tremendously blessed that Debbie had introduced me to this valuable tool which had gently enabled me to navigate and heal some of my other life encounters. Those that were relevant to my need to heal from my cnacer.

After my QHHT session, I was extremely excited and happy to share with John and also with my spiritual group how deeply profound and healing the experience was. This session with Debbie had opened the door to something bigger than my conscious self.

I instinctively knew that I still needed more healing work on unresolved issues from past lives and this current life. This required me to delve deeper into my subconscious for the benefit of my emotional and spiritual wellbeing. The healing that had commenced at the powerful session with Debbie was the start of something significant in my journey to wellness. I was now aware that I needed to heal myself on many layers. I still had so much more to uncover and to learn.

A few days after the intense session with Debbie, I carried out my own self-hypnosis. Whilst lying awake in my bed early one morning at precisely 2.22am, I managed to enter my subconscious by relaxing my body and mind sufficiently into a somnambulistic state so that I could 'explore' the purpose of the tumour in my left breast.

In my subconscious, I was able to travel within my own body and locate the tumour. Once I was within the mass of the tumour I had the ability to gain a direct understanding of the root of the problem, to find out what the real reason for the cancer was. It was a deeply spiritual and emotional occurrence, as I could see inside my tumour and enquire why the growth had occurred. Following on from this I became aware of what was required for me to heal myself.

What I discovered through this process, helped me to understand that the issues were all within my power to heal. I simply had to believe that this was possible and send more love and healing to myself, and to my tumour.

In addition, I needed to send love and healing to unresolved situations I had encountered during my lifetimes, which had caused me immense emotional turmoil. I was truly opening to my spirit and surrendering to what I had to learn. I felt so blessed to be able to experience what was happening to me and truly saw it as a message that I needed to change my life for the better from that moment onwards.

At the next meeting of Starlight Spiritual, I eagerly shared what had happened with my trusted friends, who listened in awe and wonder as I recounted my experience.

I was on a quest, and always open to trying anything

that I genuinely considered would help me. I then happened upon some information about a practise called laughter yoga. Curious, I was aware how laughter not only makes us feel good, but it is reported to produce pain-blocking endorphins in the brain.[9] I was sure this yoga practise could do many positive things for me both psychologically as well as physically. Sitting chatting to my spiritual friends one night, I was explaining my interest in laughter yoga. Just after I had said that I would like to try it myself, Dawn turned around and exclaimed smiling, "I am qualified to teach laughter yoga!" My excitement was palpable "Wow, when can we start?" I enquired. Setting a date and time we caught up a few nights later at Dawn's house to give it a try.

I couldn't believe how easy it was to start laughing even when there didn't seem to be anything obvious to laugh about! I laughed until my cheeks hurt, and my sides ached. This felt like great therapy and was such fun.

Dawn and I proceeded to engage in laughter yoga sessions every Monday for the next few weeks. A few others joined us when they could. It was fabulous.

It is so good to laugh. This was just the additional tonic I needed. I even encouraged my mother-in-law to go with me to Dawn's house when she was visiting. It occurred to me, *I am so blessed to have such wonderful people as Debbie and Dawn working alongside me, supporting me on my journey.* These people had entered my life just at the right time.

By this time, I had come to accept the many 'coincidences' in my life and express my gratitude to the Universe for what I was receiving. These experiences were linked to, what I now realised was, very much a spiritual journey I was on.

Whilst shopping in the town centre one day, I went into Waterstones, and a book called 'The Journey' by Brandon Bays seemed to be calling out to me from the shelf. I had previously been told about this book on more than one occasion and was excited to pick it up to have a browse. I sensed that there was something I needed to learn from Brandon's story. Interestingly, there were many parts to her story that resonated with me. My gut instinct was urging me to purchase the book, and I almost ran to the till with sheer excitement. Yes, I knew that reading

Brandon's book was going to help me too.

Eager to find out more, the next day I sat down with a large glass of water ready to read Brandon's incredible story. There were no clouds in the sky; the sun was shining in its full glory. *What a superb day for September,* I ruminated. I placed one of my upright dining room chairs just inside my back door out of the draft, allowing the sun to embrace my body with its warm rays. Opening a new book and smelling the appealing aroma of the newly printed pages, always gives me such a thrill. Taking time to ease open the pages, added to the sense of excitement.

Once I started to devour Brandon's story, I didn't want to stop. It was as if she was talking directly to me. My experience with cancer and reaction to it, in many ways, mirrored her own. She was also reluctant to tell many people about her diagnosis.[10] I was intensely fascinated by her process of dealing with the emotional aspects of her tumour. Particularly as she had also gone inside her tumour in much the same way as I had done. [11]

Brandon took herself on various journeys into her

body to discover what her illness was all about and to send healing to those involved. I couldn't put the book down and decided that I had to try her journey experience myself, then and there, to see what would happen. Without really understanding why I just knew that Brandon's technique would be able to help me in some way.

I re-read the section on how she dealt with a particularly emotional issue, by taking herself into the causes of her emotions. Memorizing the process she used to explore and go down through the layers of anger, disappointment, and feelings of abandonment. The Journey takes the person experiencing it to a transition point, which for Brandon was the edge of a black hole. She likens it to a 'black void of nothingness'. [12]

As I sat there, bathed in the rays of the September sunshine, I closed my eyes and took three deep breaths to relax. Within a few moments, I was able to take my awareness into my body, to discover the predominant emotion which felt as it if was 'lodged' there. The process of self-hypnosis was a natural next step for me, because of all the other experiences

I had gone through in the previous few weeks. I took myself down through the layers of emotion as Brandon had described in her book, enquiring each time to myself what lay beyond each one in turn. The feelings that emitted as I experienced each emotion were so intense.

The process was extremely powerful as it played out so easily for me in the initial stages. I was undergoing strong emotions of anger, disappointment, and sadness. Then I reached the metaphorical 'black hole'. For me, it was like a vortex that was swirling before me. I remembered how Brandon said that she waited there for a long time before taking the plunge. I decided that if I spent too long at this place, I would not be able to proceed. There was no one to encourage me, so I had to be resolute. The whole episode was intensely emotional. I was beginning to have serious doubts about my ability to see the process through. I, therefore, resolved not to hesitate any longer and I 'jumped' directly into the swirling black mass.

Oh, my God, what have I done? My thoughts were all over the place, as the all-consuming blackness was swirling around me for what seemed like an eternity.

The dark vortex seemed to be suffocating me. My emotions poured out as I screamed and cried. My dog Lenny was running around my feet, whining, then putting his paw on my knee and nudging me with his nose.

Lenny's actions were a great comfort to me, keeping me grounded. He rescued me from feeling completely alone in my self-imposed prison. I honestly do not know how long I was in this state of fear and helplessness; it seemed to be going on forever. Then somehow, magically, I emerged from the blackness into a feeling of complete joy. I felt unequivocally happy and joyful with no fear or worry. I let these feelings wash over me, seemingly cleansing me of my negative emotions.

In my curiosity, I enquired what lay beyond joy. I then experienced total peace, with an intensity I am unable to describe. This resulted in feeling completely at peace with everything and everyone. So, was there anything beyond peace? I opened my consciousness up to what was beyond the peace. It was love. The experience was one of total, unconditional love, which lay beyond the conscious mind. A feeling so deep and profound that I am unable to put it into words. It was of such a high vibration. I simply had to check, *What is beyond Love?*' The answer came immediately, *Nothing. God is Love.* I felt as if I had complete and absolute knowing and understanding. A tacit knowledge that can never be achieved through thought alone, this was a knowing that emitted from deep within my heart.

From that day to this I have described my cancer diagnosis as a blessing and sent love and thanks to my tumour for providing the necessary 'wakeup call' to allow me to change my life path. I felt as if my foot was suddenly on the accelerator pedal of my existence. What had previously been a slow and often interrupted Spiritual Path, had simply become a roller coaster ride. It was the ride of my life!

Not content with discovering what I had learned from this experience, I used Brandon's process to delve deeper and venture into my subconscious a few more times. I knew that this was helping me to heal and I wanted to discover what else I needed to work on. This has proved an invaluable tool in my overall healing on an emotional, mental as well as spiritual level.

All these situations and many more made me realise how easily we can attract exactly what we need into our lives at just the right time.

Chapter 6

Food, Supplements, Home Remedies and more

I thought I had a good diet - it just was not good enough!

I didn't eat wheat, rarely ate anything sweet, and enjoyed lots of fruit and vegetables in my diet. I seldom ate red meat, and I cooked most of my meals from scratch using fresh chicken, fish, and vegetables. I didn't rely on ready meals. *What do I need to do differently?* I pleaded with myself to come up with the solution.

First of all, I didn't eat any organic produce. Like many people I had spoken to, I simply thought that organic produce was too expensive. I was, however, aware that organic produce is better than non-organic because of the lack of pesticides. In addition, I had seen Kirlian photographs[1] showing the energy field around a piece of organic fruit, where there is none around non-organic fruit. This also highlights how we are receiving the energy from the fruit and vegetables when we eat organic. I also learned through reading books including, 'Say No to Cancer' by Patrick Holford, that there are further benefits from eating organic fruit and vegetables for a cancer-free diet.

I discovered that many types of organic fruit, vegetables, and herbs also have a lot more than simply additional vitamins and minerals that non-organic produce, they contain molecules called salvestrols. Salvestrols are generated by plants as natural insecticides and fungicides. Therefore, they are only found in organic produce, which has not been sprayed with chemicals to repel insects and fungus. Introducing salvestrols into the diet is important for anyone with a diagnosis such as mine

---

1   Kirlian photography, named after Semyon Kirlian, is a collection of photographic techniques used to capture the occurrence of energy fields around a person, animal or plant.

as they attack cancer cells. Patrick Holford covers this in detail in his book. [13]

Even now many people are curious about my diet and how it helped me to heal myself. When I explain to people that I eat as much organic fruit and vegetables as I can, the first comment most of them make is along the lines of, 'Yes, but organic fruit and vegetables and organic meat and chicken are just too expensive.' My question is then, 'what price do we put on our health and the health of our children? If we can't pay for good food, why do we shell out for all sorts of products and services that we don't really need?'

I had most likely been ingesting residue from the multitude pesticides used on fruit and vegetables without any knowledge of what they were. I then resolved to eat more organic vegetables in future, plus more leafy greens.

The chicken and beef which I had been consuming were not organic. It had most likely been injected with artificial hormones, as well as being fed on non-organic feed. Although I ate red meat only once or twice a week, I did eat chicken on a regular basis, thinking it was the healthier option.

All this was going into my body. I also ate a lot of salmon, mistakenly thinking it too was healthy. However, this is not really the case, considering that much of the salmon we consume in the UK is farmed and full of antibiotics and other nasty substances! Adding to this, on occasion when I ate something from the supermarket which has been processed in any way and included chemicals, with names that I am unable to pronounce, I was slowly poisoning my body.

When I first started my new eating regime, I initially began by cutting out the 'easy' things like tins, packets, and jars of anything that I didn't recognise or understand one or more of the ingredients mentioned on the label. Have you ever studied labels? I didn't know that there were so many strange sounding ingredients in food! In fact, the question increasingly on my mind was, *is this really food?* And *Is it nourishing my body as food should?*

I also discovered that I didn't drink enough water,

and most of the water I did drink was probably not doing me much good, due to the processing it undergoes, with chemicals added such as fluoride and chlorine. Concerns over the possible links between these chemicals and cancer are raised in Ty Bolinger's book 'The Truth About Cancer. [14]

I began to filter my drinking water from the tap and I cut out drinking water from plastic bottles because most of them contain chemicals which are also widely reported to be carcinogenic. In particular, according to Patrick Holford, "they can disrupt hormonal signals – they generally have an oestrogenic effect".[15] So for me, as my cancer had been diagnosed as oestrogen positive, avoiding as many soft plastics as possible was 'a given'.

Ideally, I would have liked a filter tap, which I did have installed a few months later. In the meantime, I had to do with filling my filter jug which was in constant use.

One of the biggest culprits, which should be excluded from the diet of anyone with cancer, is sugar. I didn't consciously add refined sugar to my food or drinks, however, it was present in most processed foods, even many savoury dishes that you wouldn't expect, such as curry sauces. My consumption of such foods was low. There were times, however, when I had been busy and without thinking, had resorted to eating supermarket ready meals or pre-prepared jars of sauce for convenience. Not a big eater of sweet treats, I had still indulged in the occasional cake or biscuit accompanied by a cup of instant coffee, to 'keep me going'.

Up until this point, I did partake in enjoying home baking particularly as one of my daughters, Melissa, loves to bake. This was probably the hardest thing of all to give up, as I knew how much effort she had put into creating her delicious cakes and biscuits. All the books I have now read on alternative and complimentary treatments for cancer mention the dangers of refined sugar; it is even publicised on the news and in magazine articles. In effect 'sugar feeds cancer'. According to Andreas Mortiz, in his book 'Cancer is not a Disease,' sugar is one of their (cancer cells) favourite energy supplying foods. [16] I was resolute in my decision; SUGAR HAD TO GO!

Another offender was dairy. Although I didn't drink milk, I did add it to my coffee and was quite partial to cappuccino, which contains a sizeable portion of milk in each cup. I also ate a lot of cheese, particularly hard cheddar cheeses.

What I discovered was that dairy is particularly bad for those who have breast cancer, principally because cows' milk contains high levels of growth-inducing hormones including oestrogen. Patrick Holford explains this in his book 'Say No to Cancer, referring to a survey of over 55,000 people which was the largest ever health and diet survey in the UK. The results of which, "found that the more milk a person drinks, the worse their overall health, their digestion, immune and hormonal health", suggesting that, "many of us are not well suited to drinking milk – and perhaps that includes you." [17]

Finding substitutes for some of what I had cut out of my diet, was sometimes difficult. I tried a branded coconut milk from the supermarket, only to discover that it has sugar in it! It seemed best to just change my eating habits, to eliminate the need for milk and cheese, rather than trying to introduce substitutes.

However, the more I read and researched about the effects of certain foods on our bodies, the more I realised that much of what I had been eating had not helped my health.

I then had a drastic rethink about my diet and decided that I should go *back to basics*. I cut out everything that was in any way processed or considered to be detrimental to those who have cancer. I then ended up with vegetables, fruit, nuts, seeds, and legumes as my staple diet. This was challenging at first, not just because I missed some of what I used to eat, but because I had a family to cook for as well.

On the positive side, I now had the ability to introduce them to the wonders of organic fruit and vegetables. I didn't, however, expect them to have a strict diet like mine. After all, my body had a big job to do to repair my damaged immune system, which I believed had been partly responsible for the cancer which had been growing inside of me.

I spent quite a bit of time discussing my new diet with my friend Debbie. Being a vegan herself, she gave me some hints and tips on ensuring that I had sufficient vitamins and minerals in my diet. I wanted to get most of my nutrition from what I ate rather than relying too heavily on supplements.

I also referred to books for tips on the changes I needed to make. One book which I have had for years by Gillian McKeith called 'You Are What You Eat' had loads of valuable information in it on vitamins and minerals, and which foods were best sources of these. In particular, she goes into a lot of detail on what is referred to as 'superfoods'.[18]

The cornerstone of my new eating regime was juicing fresh, organic vegetables, which I drank every day. Juicing is a perfect way to get nutrients into your system quickly because the body does not use valuable energy digesting food to benefit from them. My juicer, which John bought me for Christmas a few years earlier, had become my new best friend! The juices were simple, mainly carrot, celery, beetroot, ginger and garlic with a few pinches of turmeric and a dash of olive oil or flaxseed oil. 'Garlic contains around 200 biologically active compounds, many of which protect against cancer.' [19]

The remainder of my diet, in the early days after my diagnosis, consisted of eating mostly raw or steamed vegetables with some beans thrown in for essential protein. The key ingredients being organic. I snacked on fresh organic fruit, nuts, and seeds on occasion when I was hungry. Most of the time my new diet left me feeling full and satisfied. Interestingly, I didn't crave sugar, as many people do when they go on diets. I didn't consider what I was doing to be dieting. I was simply making necessary changes to what I ate to detoxify my body and boost my immune system. I didn't feel as if I denied myself anything, as I relished the delicious food I was introducing to my body.

I was delighted that I had discovered the importance of these molecules called salvestrols found in many organic foods and how they even attack cancer cells. As a result, I was adding as many organic foods containing these essential molecules as possible, including apples, blackberries, broccoli and more. Interestingly I found some late ripening blackberries one day whilst out on my walk with Lenny. After that, I took along a small container and picked a few handfuls each time I went for a walk.

I had no strong desire to lose weight, as I had never considered my weight to be a problem. I never really thought of myself as overweight, and I didn't weigh myself on a regular basis. Interestingly, although I knew that I was not my ideal weight, I had had a 'health check' at my local gym some months earlier when the fitness instructor who was carrying it out labelled me 'obese.' Upon hearing that, I fathomed that the system was wrong, as I saw myself as reasonably fit and was not physically restricted by my weight. *No,* I concluded, *at ten stone, I am certainly not obese.*

Following that encounter, I knew that I was around ten stone at the time of my diagnosis, give or take a few pounds. When my altered eating habits resulted in me starting to lose weight, I simply knew by my clothes which were becoming far too big for me. Interestingly, I did lose around two stone in weight, as I went down from a size 14 to a size 10. I was amazed that I had done this by merely eating different food, rather than eating less. I certainly didn't feel as if I was dieting in the traditional sense of the word, I had simply changed my diet, as I had never been someone who wanted to deprive myself to get thinner.

Despite these beliefs, once I became used to my new figure, I realised how much unnecessary weight I had been carrying, and how much better I felt without it. Losing weight was definitely a positive by-product of my new regime. I felt good with my new body shape which contributed to my overall feelings of wellness and energy. Feelings which were emerging as the days and weeks passed.

It wasn't just the organic vegetables and fruit which made a difference; I also began to use more herbs and spices in my cooking. Particularly one spice, which I never use sparingly, is turmeric. The main active component in turmeric is curcumin which is known as a phytonutrient. Patrick Holford refers to various studies into the benefits of turmeric and how curcumin has been shown to inhibit cancer growth.[20] In essence, curcumin possesses anti-cancer effects, as well as displaying antioxidant, anti-viral, anti-inflammatory, anti-bacterial and anti-fungal properties.

A very special herb (as well as a spice), which can always be seen growing on my windowsill now, is coriander. Coriander has many benefits, and it contains dietary fibre, manganese, iron, and magnesium. Coriander is a simple, natural way to detoxify the body and remove toxic heavy metals like mercury, lead, and cadmium from tissues. This was investigated in a study carried out by Dr. Yoshiaki Omura for the Heart Disease Research Foundation in New York. Omura found that the leaves of the coriander plant accelerated the excretion of mercury, lead, and aluminium from the body.[21]

There was also a place for essential oils in my new regime and one particular oil, in the early days was frankincense. Although I was focussing on improving my immune system through diet and exercise, I knew that I also had to take something to try to 'kill' the cancer. I had been told about frankincense essential oil and its anti-cancer properties. In general, all essential oils are vitally important as they, 'contain compounds that stop angiogenesis, or the growth of veins and arteries, in cancer tumours.' [22]

Principally frankincense is said to demonstrate

particularly strong anti-cancer properties. Interestingly frankincense is mentioned in the Bible, as the 'Three Wise Men' presented it as a gift to the baby Jesus. Therefore, I fathomed that it was certainly good enough for me!

I discovered that, as with many of the remedies I tried, the facts appeared to show that frankincense had helped people to heal from cancer. However, much of the evidence was anecdotal and had not been tested on sufficient numbers of people to be 'proven.' This is true of the studies referred to in Ty Bollinger's book 'The Truth about CANCER'.[23] Interestingly, I had met someone who had regularly used frankincense as part of his anti-cancer regime, so decided to research the possible benefits. I figured that it was worth trying, to see if it could help me.

I started using the frankincense gradually at first by drinking three drops diluted in water morning and evening. I then progressed onto taking it neat, by taking three drops directly under my tongue. I also rubbed it directly onto my left breast. I continued with this part of my regime for a few weeks, until the day I realised that I no longer needed to use it. My body told me that it was no longer necessary, as my mouth started to tingle after I inserted the drops. Leaving it for a few days, I tried again with the same result. The same happened with the skin on my breast, which then came up in a small rash. I then knew it was time to move on. I was also feeling much stronger by then, as many of the initial side effects of my detox regime had subsided. I still occasionally used frankincense it in my bath, so that I could inhale the fragrance and benefit from it in a diluted form.

I also started taking vitamin D3 which is often deficient in those with cancer, and started supplementing my diet with a range of vitamins, nutrients, and minerals, including, coenzyme Q10 (CoQ10), zinc, folic acid and B vitamins. However, after receiving the results of some blood tests I had carried out through my GP, I decided that I was probably getting sufficient vitamins and minerals from the food I was eating, therefore, I didn't need to take all of these. Interestingly, my folate levels were higher than normal, which was probably due to all the leafy green vegetables in my diet.

My interest in CoQ10 came initially from a talk I attended at the Harry Edwards Healing Centre. At this talk, a lady had explained how she had been diagnosed with a tumour on her lung, and she had supplemented with the antioxidant CoQ10 along with several other remedies. CoQ10, which is actually classed as a nutrient and not a vitamin, helps to protect cells from carcinogens, as well as helping to recycle Vitamin E.[24] Studies have shown that those with cancer can be deficient in CoQ10. I began to supplement with CoQ10 and continued to take it throughout my healing process.

Around this time, I also came across some information on the possible link between lack of iodine and incidence of individuals with breast cancer. Interestingly, Ty Bollinger reports that "fluoride supplants iodine in the thyroid gland, a contributing factor to thyroid cancer".[25] (I have previously also referred to the suggested link between fluoride and cancer.)

Iodine deficiency was something I had never considered. Although I was aware of iodine and its link to the thyroid gland, I didn't fully appreciate that it may be important for me to check if I was deficient, due to the suspected connection between low iodine levels and cancer. I studied all I could find on the internet on iodine deficiency and the link between iodine deficiency and various illnesses, including breast cancer.

If it was true that there was a possible link between iodine deficiency and cancer, particularly in those with breast cancer. The question on my mind at the time was, *Why do doctors not check iodine levels?*

I asked my GP for an iodine test, only to be told that it was not available! I still didn't have an answer to my question. I researched and purchased the type of iodine I could ingest safely and did a self-test to see if I was deficient. This consisted of simply painting a circle of iodine on my inner arm and leaving it for 'up to 24 hours', to see what happened. It disappeared immediately!! As I appeared to be severely deficient, I needed no further convincing and proceeded to supplement with iodine as part of my daily regime.

Another 'supplement' I took daily consisted of crushed apricot kernels. The key thing about apricot kernels is they are deemed to kill cancer cells. Patrick Holford explains how apricot kernels can benefit those with cancer, "An extract from the apricot kernel, laetrile has often been used in aggressive anti-cancer strategies. It acts more like chemotherapy and is claimed to target only the cancer cells." [26]

One particularly important part of my daily regime from early on was a 'home remedy' that is relatively cheap and easily available. After doing my research, I started taking bicarbonate of soda with lemon. The primary reason for this remedy was to keep my digestive system in an alkaline state with a PH of 7 or more. I discovered that maintaining the correct acid/alkaline balance was crucial to my detox programme.[27] In addition, high acidity in the body can cause cellular metabolism to cease, resulting in oxygen deprivation. Cancer prefers low oxygen environments.[28] I religiously tested my urine every morning with PH test sticks, to check how alkaline my body was. I then regulated my intake of bicarbonate of soda accordingly. I did this because much of my diet was alkaline forming and I did not want my body to be too alkaline either.

Around a month after my diagnosis, aided by my friend Vincaine who is a homeopathic practitioner, I tried some homeopathic remedies to help my healing process.[2] The two remedies which I tried were Conium 30c and Carcinosinum 200c. Conium is a remedy for tumours, and Carcinosinum is prescribed to detox cancer patients, or to prevent cancer in patients with a family history of cancer.

I genuinely feel that taking them played a part in my healing process; although how much it is difficult to measure exactly. I took them on alternate weeks for a total of three weeks, starting and ending with a course of Conium. When I first tried to take the Conium, which I had to dilute in water, I felt really tired. I knew that sometimes homeopathic remedies could make us feel slightly worse when we initially

take them, so I persevered. Liking it to the analogy of clearing out a room, whereby the room always looks worse before it gets better. And it is always

---

2   Complete Homeopathy   (Vincianne Ollington)
http://www.completehomeopathy.co.uk/

worth it in the end! As if to prove the point, I felt markedly better after the three weeks were over. My head felt clearer, and I had more energy to help me get through the day. I believe that the homeopathic remedies were helpful to me in the early days after my diagnosis. I was confident to take them because, as they are diluted many times, they simply give the energy of the substance. This is much gentler on the system than taking prescription drugs.

Later in my regime, I heard about Essiac tea. It comes from a native American Indian recipe which is deemed to help those who are taking an alternative cancer route. You can read about this herbal concoction in Ty Bollinger's book, 'The Truth About Cancer'. [29] As I was unable to source the Essiac tea locally, I had it shipped over from Canada. It has a herbal flavour which is rather pleasant. Once I started taking it, I certainly felt much more energetic. Whether it was the tea or my new regime in general, I am unable to say.

In addition to ensuring that I had the correct diet and supplements that I needed, I was aware that I needed to rid my body of all the bad toxins that had built up over the years. From airborne pollutants to harmful chemicals in the non-organic food, I had been eating, my toxic load was probably elevated to the extreme. Particularly, as in addition to the usual toxins ingested by people daily, I had been exposed to fumes from aviation fuel on a daily basis. I had worked for fourteen years at airports, and aviation fuel is particularly carcinogenic. I considered that this had probably elevated my levels of toxicity to a greater level than average for a woman of my age. Eliminating the toxins was something I was acutely aware that I must do.

I knew that I needed to do more than just change my diet to achieve success in the detox part of my regime. That is when I realised the wonders of the coffee enema. I had come across the use of coffee enemas for cancer patients from many different sources, including Laura Bond's book, 'Mum's NOT Having Chemo'.[30] This book was lent to me by a friend of mine. As there was so much valuable information in it, I purchased my own copy to keep and use for reference.

The idea of administering coffee enemas to cancer

patients was well documented by Dr. Max Gerson, who dispensed them to his patients. This was a key element of his 'Guerson Therapy' protocol as far back as the 1930's.[31] Guerson's therapy was devised by him initially as a cure for his own migraines. It was essentially a nutrition-based programme, which Max Guerson later used predominantly with patients who were suffering from either cancer or diabetes. Interestingly, the use of enemas to aid the healing process was not a new idea, in fact, there is evidence of enemas being used by the Egyptians far back as 1500BC.[32]

The Guerson Therapy in general, and in particular coffee enemas, have been followed by many cancer sufferers who chose non-conventional healing routes, plus those who opt for a mix of conventional and natural healing methods.[33] I had investigated the diet that goes with the Guerson Therapy but had discounted it due to the fact that some of the key ingredients in the diet were things that I no longer ate, including white potatoes. This is another reminder that there is no 'one size fits all' solution to help someone when they are trying to heal from an illness. I strongly believe that there is a lot of common ground in what cancer sufferers and others with serious health conditions should eat. The exact remedies and specific diet, however, needs to be tailored precisely to each person, as everyone is unique.

The coffee enema, however, had cropped up in other research that I had read, and in fact, enemas were used in hospitals in the UK up until recent years, and they were well known to help patient recovery.

I deliberated on the advantages of coffee enemas for some time, before I plucked up the courage to administer one to myself. I had ordered the enema kit online a few weeks before, along with some obscure coffee to go with it that appeared to be coming from the Philippines! "Why?" you may ask. When I ordered the kit, somehow this was the coffee that had been bought previously by others who ordered enema kits. I didn't really research it enough at the time; I just assumed that I needed special coffee. Anyway, it turns out that I could use any medium roast filter coffee, provided it was organic. Upon realising this, I had run out of excuses, and two months into my regime, I compelled myself to give it a try.

Before commencing with the treatment, I went through the instructions I had read in detail. I did not want to miss anything vital to the success of the procedure. After all, this type of activity was quite alien to me at the time. I knew I had run out of excuses, so all I had to do was give it a try.

The kit itself seemed easy enough to assemble. As I had been considering using it for some time before I plucked up the courage to give it a go. What really helped me was talking to a couple of people who had successfully used coffee enemas to aid in their self-healing. One of whom explained in detail what I needed to do. In her book, Laura Bond also goes into the process of giving oneself a coffee enema.[34] I read, and reread the instructions on the procedure before I started, keen to 'get it right'.

I allocated at least an hour for my first session and timed it when there was no one else in the house. Inserting the enema tube was challenging, however, the thought was much worse than the reality. Retaining the coffee for up to 15 minutes was by far the hardest part of the process. Most days I managed 9 to 12 minutes. Deep breathing and a belief that what I was doing would help my body to rid itself of the toxins that had built up over the years enabled me to continue with the unusual procedure.

I persisted with my practise daily for over three months, until I had the feeling that I no longer needed to do so. I then cut back to once a week, which seemed to work for me. This then became part of my ongoing routine.

As time went on, I became acutely aware that not only had I had problems with what I was putting in my body in the way of food, I was also adding to my toxic load by the chemicals I was lathering onto my face and body on a regular basis.

For years I had used body lotion religiously every day after my shower to soften my skin. I also used all manner of products such as make-up, deodorant and sun creams. After studying the contents of what was in these products, much of which I could not even pronounce, let alone understand what they were; these all had to go. One day I simply opened my make-up purse, bedroom drawers and bathroom cabinet and cleared them of every single body and face product. The face cream, the body lotion, the deodorant and even my toothpaste had to go. I started from scratch with the essentials including coconut oil and a body brush for dry brushing. Interestingly, my skin is softer today than it was when I lathered all the chemically laden products onto it without thinking.

Another great method of detoxification for me was indulging myself by relaxing in a Himalayan salt bath. This helped to draw the toxins out of my skin, as well as helping to relax my mind and my body. The magnesium in the salts which is an extremely beneficial mineral. 'Magnesium is essential for over 300 functions of the body.' [35] It is always lovely to lie back and enjoy the relaxing feeling of the warm water on my body. A real treat for relaxing both the body and the mind!

Chapter 7

Reiki and Mindfulness

Essential tools for my self-healing.

I had been practising and teaching Reiki for self-healing and for healing others for many years, and it featured greatly in my daily regime.

As previously mentioned, I had received spiritual and energy healing from a number of sources, particularly in the early days after my diagnosis. At that time, I needed healing to calm my nerves and help me to release the shock and stress I was experiencing. In the subsequent days and weeks, healing helped me, as I came to terms with the necessary changes in my life.

In addition to receiving healing from the Harry Edwards Healing Centre, I was also receiving healing sent by my mother-in-law, Philo's prayers. My sister and some of my friends were also sending me various forms of distant and spiritual healing. I could often feel when I was receiving the healing during the night or, more precisely, in the early hours of the morning as I lay in bed. When this happened, my body would move involuntarily as if being manipulated, and my breathing would become deeper and slower. This was often accompanied by a feeling of tingling all over my body. It generally started around 3.33am and went on for approximately 40 minutes. During these nightly sessions, I felt so calm, so loved and so blessed. This healing also helped me emotionally, as it was accompanied by an inner knowing that *everything is going to be okay.*

I regularly treated myself to some Reiki energy as part of my own self-healing. Much of this was in the form of healing meditations, using ancient sounds called Kotodama that invoke aspects of physical, mental, emotional and spiritual healing. In addition, I regularly carried out hands-on healing on myself, particularly at bedtime. Placing my hands on my heart and solar plexus helped to relax me. I could feel the healing heat from my own hands penetrate through my skin and deep into my body.

Interestingly, Mrs. Hawayo Takata, who was instrumental in bringing Reiki to the West from Japan in the 1930's, was said to have learned this healing technique after being cured of her own multiple illnesses.[36] In my personal experience, I have seen many positive changes in people who receive regular Reiki treatments, because the healing energy of Reiki, as with other forms of energy healing, can be extremely powerful.

I had been introduced to Reiki on one memorable occasion, by my sister, Carolyne, when I was living in Glasgow many years before. Carolyne explained that she had learned the technique and that it was much like a form of Spiritual hands-on healing. She treated my abdomen one Christmas morning after I had experienced a severe case of food poisoning. I was due to drive us to our mother and father's house that day for Christmas lunch. However, as I had severe stomach cramps, I felt unable to drive anywhere. After the treatment, not only could I drive the 80 miles, I was also able to eat some of my Christmas lunch!

I was extremely grateful to my sister, for helping me to enjoy that Christmas. Afterwards I didn't really think much more about how Carolyne had helped me to feel better. I was just happy that it had worked at the time. In those days, I was fortunate that I normally experienced good health.

My next encounter with Reiki was in 2007 during a particularly difficult period in my life. I was suffering from the stress of juggling my challenging career and bringing up two young children.

My life was no longer my own, particularly as my female boss at work had become even more demanding since I returned to work after my second maternity leave. Dealing with challenges at work, coupled with the needs of my two young girls, became an almost impossible struggle. In my heart, I really wanted to spend more time with my girls and less at work. I put this down to a mothering instinct which emitted from deep within my subconscious. It was not a cognisant decision. This made it especially hard for me, as I instinctively felt drawn to full-time motherhood.

My head, meanwhile, was telling me that I was a career woman who had spent many years working hard to achieve the status and seniority of my position as a senior manager. This dichotomy seemed like a riddle, which I was simply unable to resolve logically. Trying to balance the two, I discovered, was impossible for me. However, I was unable to accept the reality of giving up work. It was like staring into a bottomless chasm, rendering me incapable of proceeding. Not knowing what I would encounter, if indeed there would be any light at the end of this black abyss.

I know many working mothers have had to face similar dilemmas, however at the time I felt very alone; as my work requirements became more onerous, and my previous drive and passion for my career were dissipating. This left only the deep-seated fear that I would be unable to manage if I lost this source of income. These thoughts, coupled with the realisation that the needs of my two girls would increase as they got older, were causing me a great deal of internally generated stress.

When the elder of my two girls started school, the

juggling became almost impossible. My friend Ann had explained to me, "It will get more difficult when the children go to school." She had been correct; I felt the challenge literally *smothering me*. I was living life on a knife-edge with no respite for me.

After a particularly stressful time at work, things went from bad to worse. I was finding myself awake during the night and incredibly tired during the day, walking around exhausted, almost in a dream-like state. Except this was more like a nightmare than a sedate dream: functioning, just, but not really engaged fully with anything. I spent hours when I should be sleeping, thinking about various scenarios and what I could or should do to resolve my situation to relieve the stress I was under.

Finally, with no end in sight, I made an appointment with the doctor. Hesitantly, I described my symptoms, namely not sleeping and tired all the time, with no energy and struggling to get through the day. I felt rather foolish, to be honest, as if somehow, I should not be there. It seemed like a weakness in me to admit that I was unable to cope with my life when so many other working mothers appeared to me to have everything under control.

The GP looked up briefly from his notes and stated in an authoritative voice, "I am going to put you on a course of anti-depressants because I think you are depressed!" In my desperation, and with the belief that the doctor knew what he was talking about, I collected my pills from the chemist. Even as I did so, something in the back of my mind was troubling me, *I am not sure exactly how anti-depressants will fix the problems in my life.* Upon reading the leaflet, I discovered that one of the side effects of the pills was that they could possibly make me "suicidal".

Oh, my God, my mind had gone into overdrive, *I know I am seriously stressed, but I feel I have so much to live for with two young children – I only want to feel better, not worse!* In that moment of panic, I threw the pills in the bin – I was resolute in my decision, *There must be another way?*

Fortunately, in late November 2007, I had another encounter with Reiki. This time it was to dramatically change my life and begin to change how I looked at myself and the world around me.

My sister-in-law Yvonne was visiting from Ireland. Yvonne - who was studying art at college - and I, always had a lot to talk about. With her engaging smile and cropped blond hair, she was radiating enthusiasm about this healing technique, called Reiki, which she had just learned. Yvonne explained, "I can help you switch off and feel more relaxed." "That would be a challenge." I joked. "I'm serious, I've been taught an ancient Japanese healing system called Reiki which is great for stress reduction." Although I was dubious, I vaguely recalled the healing my sister had given me that Christmas morning many years before. That, coupled with Yvonne's enthusiasm, helped to convince me. I was willing to give it a try.

I felt relaxed within a few minutes of lying down on a fluffy blanket which we had spread on my lounge floor, as Yvonne set to work. She placed her hands lightly on various areas of my head and body. I was astounded that I could feel a distinctive heat which seemed to be coming from Yvonne's hands. I likened it to having a warm hot water bottle placed on my body, wherever she laid them. It felt comforting, and I was feeling more relaxed than I had in years. The sensations evoking a feeling of relaxation, seemingly urging me to sound "aaahhh" out loud. It reminded me of the feeling I have had when sitting wrapped in a warm, cosy blanket, enjoying a hot drink, after returning home on a cold winter's day.

A whole hour elapsed, which felt like 10 minutes to me. Yvonne quietly enquired, "How are you feeling now"? Replying in a quite voice, "Thank you so much, I can't remember the last time I felt so relaxed." I hugged her, my gratitude showing on my smiling face.

I resolved to have more Reiki treatments. It was wonderful how easily it enabled me to 'switch off', live in and ENJOY the moment. With this passionate determination, I set about finding if there was anyone locally who practised Reiki. Driven by how much better the Reiki treatment made me feel, I knew that I wanted to learn how to practise Reiki myself. Within a few weeks, I had enrolled on a Reiki course. My intention was solely to learn the basics of Reiki so that I could help myself. I simply wanted to enjoy more of the relaxing, healing benefits I experienced in that wonderful session with Yvonne.

Although my initial intention was to mainly work on myself, only two months after my Reiki course I found myself studying for Reiki II. Once I had completed my Reiki II course, I was qualified to treat others outside my immediate family and circle of interested friends. It was an exciting prospect for me to introduce others to the many benefits of this type of energy healing. Completing these courses back in 2008 started my journey of self-discovery and healing, and I have been practising Reiki meditations ever since.

I also attended my Reiki Master's regular monthly Reiki shares to enjoy the experience of sharing my Reiki, as well as chatting to like-minded people. In addition I met up regularly and shared Reiki with Gwyneth, whom I had met on my Reiki II course. We used to meet almost every week at her place or mine and give each other a treatment, followed by a cup of tea and chat. A strong friendship soon formed between us; I so enjoyed sharing with Gwyneth. One day she told me that she had decided to move back to Wales to be near her family. Although I completely understood why she was moving, I missed our catch-ups immensely.

As I had developed a love of helping others by giving them Reiki treatments, in 2010 I decided to study for my Reiki Master/Teacher qualification. I hadn't previously expected to want to do this, however, it seemed the right time. I wasn't really looking to teach; I was interested in taking my Reiki practise to the next level. I wanted to discover more, as it was making such a positive difference to my life. I was a much calmer individual and was less easily stressed by external factors in my life.

After I attained my Reiki Master/Teacher qualification, I started helping my Reiki Master, Sue, at her regular shares. This helped me to build my confidence for when I started teaching. I began slowly by teaching a few of my friends. Things then changed dramatically for me when Sue confided in me that she had decided to give up teaching. She asked if I would be interested in replacing her as the teacher for Surrey with her contact, Taggart King. Taggart runs a company called Reiki Evolution, which offers Reiki courses all over the country. I was honoured that she considered asking me.

I remember the day vividly, as I was walking on St. Andrews beach with the autumn sun beating down on my face, listening to the squawking seagulls overhead when she telephoned me. I considered that the Universe was nudging me to move forward. I readily accepted, not really considering what it would mean. I try to work on the principle that we tend to regret more the opportunities we turn down in life than those we accept. Once the reality of what I had agreed to sank in I was feeling nervous but elated; I just knew this would be good for my Reiki and for me. I discovered that I especially enjoyed teaching others so that they and their friends and families could also benefit from this wonderful energy healing.

My passion for Reiki and the difference my practise has made to my life, fills me with a warm glow inside when I think about it. So much so, that at one stage, I wanted to share this with everyone else that I knew, so they could also experience the benefits. However, I discovered that only when people are ready to change can they be helped. Everyone needs to find their own way. Since then I have worked on the premise that if someone needs me, they will find me. I do not advertise my services, and yet still my clients come.

My Reiki practise was, therefore, another key part of my healing journey. I regularly treated myself and engaged in my various Reiki meditations. In addition to any physical healing I was receiving from the Reiki energy, it had a beneficial effect on my mind-set. The Reiki energy helped to keep me believing that *everything will be okay*. Even when my husband, John was focussing on the negative and trying to persuade me to follow the conventional treatment route suggested by the doctors. In my heart I now knew that had the strength to follow my own wisdom.

My interest in mindfulness grew out of my belief in, and love of, Reiki. Being mindful is such a big part of Reiki practise. I had been curious to discover more about recent teachings by Jon Kabat- Zin, which appeared to be bringing meditation practise more into the mainstream. I attended a couple of introductory sessions which piqued my interest in attending an eight-week mindfulness course. I also knew some people who were already involved with modern mindfulness practise as developed by Kabat-Zin. When I discovered that a course was being run in Woking, I decided to clear my diary so that I could enrol and attend all eight weeks. That was the beginning of another incredible chapter for me. The idea of living more mindfully definitely appealed to me.

A year later, a friend whom I had met on my eight-week course told me that she was thinking about attending a teacher training programme in mindfulness. Having previously looked into the possibility of doing this; I had discounted it on the basis that I would have to travel to either Oxford or Bangor to attend. The exciting thing about the programme that my friend was talking about was that it was being run at a retreat in Woking. This seemed like the opportunity I had been looking for. After a great deal of thought, I enrolled; attending the retreat in August 2015, only a few weeks before I received my cancer diagnosis.

During this teacher training course in mindfulness, I discovered much about my own mindfulness practise as well as learning how to teach the eight-week course. Attending the course at that time, I believe was beneficial to me as it aided how I worked through my year of healing. I simply took each day as it came not thinking about the past and what had happened yesterday, or focussing on the future and what was going to happen next. I didn't consider the enormity of what I wanted to achieve or how exactly it would happen; I concentrated on doing what I could day by day. I was simply engaged with what was happening each day at a time, each moment savouring the good things that were coming to pass for me, and doing what I could to help myself heal.

Mindfulness increasingly featured strongly in my daily routine during those crucial months of my healing regime, and now plays an immense part in my daily life. Gratefully, I was embracing the theory of Mindfulness in all its glory. I had turned towards my tumour and my diagnosis with love and acceptance. I hadn't tried to fight or run away. I had softened into the situation with love and compassion. That is truly when the MAGIC happened.

I believe categorically that my Mindfulness training and experience, plus my years of practising Reiki enabled me to find that place where life is lived in the *now* because that is all we truly have. Life is made up of those *now* moments. It's not about striving to change into someone else before we can love and heal ourselves, it is simply to be who we truly are in each moment.

How I relished this knowledge, and made it my truth. Isn't it ironic that sometimes it is the simple things in life which are the most powerful? The truth I experienced was that love is much more potent than fear, and that is a message I want to share with the world. Striving to change things had no place inside the peace within my heart. The wisdom of many thousands of years was being accepted and experienced by me on my journey to love.

Chapter 8

Moving From 'Shelf Help' to 'Self-Help'

Putting the theory into practise

I had been reading self-help books for many years. I knew a lot of the theory of physical, spiritual and emotional healing by eating healthily and changing the way I looked at life through loving myself unconditionally. Although many of the ideas I had read about were not necessarily difficult to understand, putting the theory into practice is what made it particularly testing. Most of us know what we should be eating and spending our time doing. It's the implementation we often find difficult. It was time for me to employ what I knew; to practise more of what I had been teaching over the past few years.

I needed to implement the ethos of the Eat-Breathe-Love workshops that I had once run in conjunction with Janet, a nutritional therapist and Judith, a 'breath work' practitioner. I had to become one with all I knew. In the same way I had discovered that Reiki was so much more than teaching and healing others, with some self-meditation. Although I regularly meditated, there was so much more I knew I could do, with the skills I had learned, for my own self-healing. I turned my focus on myself as I had come to realise that my diagnosis was about all aspects of me in a much bigger way than I had understood.

Whilst running the Eat-Breathe-Love workshops, I was affectionately known as the 'Love Yourself Lady' because much of my message was about how important self-love is to our health. Even after we disbanded Eat-Breathe-Love, I was still running mini workshops on self-love and how important it is to our wellbeing. Upon receiving my diagnosis, I initially considered this to be a bit ironic.

Again, and again the common theme through most of what I was reading was the need for self-love. This was exactly what I had been teaching at my workshops. In the early days, after my diagnosis, I questioned myself, *What new information do I need to learn, and how much of what I know do I simply need to put into practise?*

I likened myself to a plumber with a leaky tap at home. I knew what I should be doing, and I was using my skills to help others. However, although I had always endeavoured to 'walk my talk', it was obvious to me that there was much more I needed to do for myself. This realisation brought me back to accepting that I was on my journey, and this was simply another lesson that I had to learn.

Yes, I had been walking my talk for many years with my Reiki, combined with the conscious effort I made to consider my feelings in my own daily life. I had also done a lot of mediation and healing work on myself. What I began to realise was that it all helped me to focus on my own self-healing, much quicker than I may otherwise have done if I had not already been on my journey of self-discovery.

There is a phrase that Jon Kabat Zin, founder of the eight-week Mindfulness-Based Stress Reduction courses, has been known to make: 'Do not start weaving your parachute when you are about to jump out of the aeroplane.' This metaphor seemed particularly pertinent at this stage. I felt so blessed that my 'parachute' was available to me when I needed it, to use Kabat Zin's analogy.

I realised that it was actually time to congratulate myself, for having to hand many of the tools I required, rather than a time to berate myself for being sick in the first place. This lesson was providing me with another opportunity to love myself even more. Many people have enquired how I found the strength to take an alternative route when the experts were giving me different advice. I put this down to having already 'woven my parachute'.

There is no one size fits all when it comes to healing. We are all unique individuals, and as such our healing journeys ought also to be individual to us. When I was doing my research, I discovered so many natural healing options; I simply couldn't do everything. At times, I had to stop researching and just focus on what I could do, one day at a time.

Some of the options I discovered were too expensive, such as going to a clinic in South America. Others were even illegal, such as using cannabis. I did briefly consider this, because of the well-documented benefits of cannabis oil. However, having two teenage daughters in the house, I discounted it for other less controversial options.

On many occasions, I simply tapped into my faith in the Universe to guide me to what would work for me.

I relished reading a lot of books during my recovery period, not just about cancer and alternative therapies. I also read spiritual books when I felt overwhelmed by the advice, sometimes conflicting, on what I should be doing to heal myself. When my brain was suffering from information overload, and I simply needed a break from it all, I took refuge in my Spiritual books by authors such as Tich Nat Han, Krishnamurti, and Wayne Dyer.

There were quotes, such as, 'The primary cause of unhappiness is never the situation but your thoughts about it.' [37] which helped to raise me up daily. They were part of my mindful living.

What I came to appreciate at that time, is that the journey of life has no particular destination, as the road goes on to infinity. Essentially, the journey is the destination in each moment in time. With this mindful observation, I had no real agenda. I knew that I wanted to be well, and not rely on doctors to tell me what I needed to do about my health. However, I was not on a quest to *fight* the cancer, or indeed fight with the doctors. As I didn't view my tumour as a threat, I genuinely believed that what I needed to do was send it love. I was not living in fear; I was living in acceptance and gratitude. I just had an inner knowing that everything would be okay if I followed my intuition and continued with my new healthy living regime.

All those books I had read over the years and all those hours I had studied were playing out for real. It was no longer about a logical understanding of the theory or a one-off experience. I was at that moment, on an experiential journey with no expectation or goal. This was life being lived day by day in all its glory. I was, and am still thankful for each moment. I feel humbled, blessed and grateful for the opportunity to be able to understand the 'magic' in this way. I call it magic, because the experience, and its repercussions, go beyond words.

Chapter 9

Monitoring My Progress

Exceeding my expectations

Even though I knew my body was healing, I continued to have my progress checked. This was particularly important for my family so that they could understand how my new regime was not only benefiting my health but also healing my cancer. I decided to undergo thermal scanning to develop a greater understanding of my general, as well as breast health.

I only wish I had known about thermal scanning before I'd had mammograms, I would never have allowed the doctors to recommend such a barbaric practice. Ironically, thermal imaging was, and still is occasionally, used by the NHS in some circumstances. So, the question in my mind is, *are things progressing in the detection and treatment of breast cancer?*

It is well known and documented that mammograms are carcinogenic, as they squash a woman's breasts and expose them to levels of radiation much higher than that of a normal x-ray. Even by doing this, limited information is given about the size of any potential tumour and how active it is.

One can only wonder why the medical profession allow this practice to continue for those who suspect they may have a tumour, and even for those who have no symptoms as a *method of early detection*. Thermal scanning is more of a *preventative measure* as it can detect abnormal activity long before a tumour can be detected on a mammogram.

It was two months since my diagnosis, and I was keen to discover what, if any, additional information a thermal scan could offer me. I was also convinced that I no longer wanted to have mammography to check my breasts, so this appeared to be a safe, reliable alternative.

On Wednesday 11th November 2016 at 4 pm and I was in Maghull, just outside Liverpool. John and

I had travelled up the day before to Chester where we stayed overnight before driving to the thermal imaging clinic to have my initial thermal scan.[3]

I knew that John was still extremely sceptical about what I was doing. However, I was grateful that he had decided to come with me to Liverpool. We had gone out for a delicious meal the night before to an Indian Restaurant which served freshly cooked vegetarian food; staying in an old hotel on the city wall overlooking the river, which was wonderful. We had such a lovely time. It was so romantic and special, like in the early days of our relationship.

After a relaxing morning shopping in Chester and walking around the city walls, we headed off towards Liverpool. The clinic, which was situated in a rustic farmhouse building surrounded by lovely countryside, was as comfortable and friendly as the welcome we received when we arrived.

---

3   Medical Thermal Imaging:
https://medscans.co.uk/

I was feeling slightly nervous, not of the process, but of what the scan was going to show. My trepidation was gone the instant I met Rosa Hughes who runs the clinic. She has such a caring personality which instantly put me at ease. What I hadn't known beforehand was that she had also previously been diagnosed with breast cancer which she had dealt with by employing natural healing methods, comparable to those I was employing myself. She kindly spent some time explaining to John the positive aspects of what I was doing, regarding her own experience and her healing journey. This really helped him to understand a lot more about what I was doing.

Somehow hearing the message from an independent source, appeared to convince John more than what I'd been able to do over the previous weeks. I am to this day exceedingly grateful to Rosa for this; she is such an inspiration.

The scan itself was relatively easy to undergo; the most challenging aspect was that I would have to wait a few days to get the results as the thermal images had to be sent to expert doctors in America for analysis. Although the expertise exists within the

National Health Service to analyse the images, the NHS does not provide this type of service to private clinics.

Overall, I felt more confident after my session, due to meeting Rosa who was a testament to the success of alternative methods of dealing with breast cancer, and how successful they could be.

The initial thermal scan images themselves would be used to set a benchmark for future scan images to be compared against. The results which were sent to me a few days later were much as I had expected. I was deemed to be "At High Risk", which is the worst reading possible.

My follow up scan was booked for three months' time, and I resolved not to focus on this or future scan results. I simply kept working on refining and tailoring my regime to enable a permanent lifestyle shift. Many of the changes I had made were to become my new way of living. They were amendments which have now become part of my daily routine. The focus was on me being healthy for the future and not just a 'means to an end' to help me heal from cancer. After all, I was enjoying the challenges presented to me and didn't, as many people would, consider them to be a chore.

My next hospital check-up and ultrasound scan was on Thursday 7th January 2016. The ultrasound technician checked his measurements four times, and even went back to the original paperwork to check how big my tumour was originally. When I asked him if there was a problem he exclaimed that the tumour was now measuring 3.6cm. It had been previously recorded as 3.8cm. I couldn't believe what I was hearing! The excitement started to rise in me from my toes, and the tingles ran all the way up my spine. Not only had the tumour stopped growing, but it had also marginally SHRUNK!! I felt a tingle of excitement from my head to my toes. Yes, what I was doing was working!!!

At the time of my original thermal scan I didn't think much about the next one, however, the time seemed to come around quickly as I had opted for around a three-month check-up. My follow up scan was held on 12th March 2016, four months after my first one.

I didn't have to travel to Liverpool this time as I had booked an appointment at the company's mobile clinic held in Godalming. I expected to see activity in my breast area, but I was hoping for an improvement over the first scan. The good news was that although I still had patches of red showing in the scan, the report said that the activity was much reduced since my first scan the previous November, in fact, there was reason to celebrate. My risk factor according to the classifications given had gone down from the highest score, 'At High Risk' (Suspicious), had missed out 'At Increased Risk' (Abnormal), and was now 'At Some Risk' (Equivocal). I was told that I didn't need to go back for another check-up for six months. Yippee!!!!

I was elated, however not quite ready to tell the world about my experience. I did, however, feel that I was now able to share my story with more people than before and started telling people as and when I felt the desire to. Most people's initial reaction was to say how sorry they were to hear my news. I always quickly let them know that I did not want or need any sympathy, as I looked upon the experience in a positive light and in no way thought fearful or sad thoughts. I truly saw my cancer experience as a blessing. I wanted to be honest with people, and perhaps inspire them in some small way to take a more positive stance when experiencing any kind of illness.

I also attended hospital for another ultrasound scan on Monday 21 June 2016. My tumour now measured 2.7cm, according to the ultrasound technician. This was a full 1.1cm smaller than back in September 2015. Once again, I felt blessed to receive such great news, which exceeded my expectations. The ultrasound technician was very matter of fact when he realised that my tumour appeared to have shrunk. I was elated. The nurse on duty also seemed to be in denial, and said that perhaps the readings were inaccurate!

I didn't care; I simply knew in my heart that my body was healing itself and it would only be a matter of time until what remained of my tumour had totally disappeared. No one was going to dissuade me from the truth.

Perhaps even more exciting was my next thermal scan, which was on 10 September 2016. Interestingly, I received the results on 15 September, exactly one year to the day of my original diagnosis! And the results were conclusive - there was no longer any activity in my left breast. "YES!" I whooped for joy, whilst staring at the results displayed on the screen of my computer. True to form for me, who as a young girl always cried with excitement on Christmas day, I sat there, and I sobbed by heart out. Excitement rippled through me until I felt as if I would burst! I had done it! I felt blessed and happy beyond words - I had done it!

Both breasts were now classified as 'At Low Risk', so, what exactly does 'At Low Risk' mean? Basically, it's 'Non-Suspicious - indicating low-grade thermal activity which is not suspicious for serious pathology'. 'Annual comparative follow-up is recommended.' This did not rule out existing non-active or encapsulated tumours. Well, I knew that I still had a lump which was my tumour, but that didn't really bother me.

The activity has stopped, and I achieved this in a year, I cried out to the Universe in excitement with tears rolling down my face. It was brilliant. I had done what those in the medical profession had said was impossible. I appeared to have healed myself, without an operation or drugs. If I could have danced on the ceiling, I would have!! Instead, I jumped on my trampette in my excitement, as Lenny ran around the house with one of my slippers in his mouth, joining in the fun. I knew he shared my happiness, as I hugged him in pure elation.

I didn't need another scan for a year!

And for those who were still sceptical about my results, citing that I still had a tumour inside of me: on January 6th, 2017 I had yet another ultrasound scan, and the ultrasound technician simply couldn't find the tumour. After referring to my previous scans on the computer, he then had another look and identified what was left of the mass. In my excitement, I enquired how big the area was. 1.4cm, at the very most. Whoop!! I was laughing, and neither the ultrasound technician nor the nurse knew quite what to say. When I exclaimed to him "it probably isn't acceptable to give you a hug", at least I received a genuine smile from them both.

What do I do now? I knew I had to tell people, but how would I do this. I had always been a private person and wasn't used to seeking attention. However, I knew I should be spreading my message, not for any personal recognition as such, but to help others. This I felt was part of my life purpose. I felt compelled to publish my story so that others could, if they wished, benefit from the learning I had experienced.

Chapter 10

Learning to Truly Love Myself

'Where there is love, fear cannot exist.'

Of all the learning which has come out of my diagnosis, this is by far the most important and far-reaching. Truly learning to love myself, my challenging side, as well as my positive traits, required me to delve deep into my soul and accept myself as I truly am. As mentioned previously, this is something I have been working on for a few years. Many texts refer to the importance of loving ourselves, and it is said in many teachings old and new. Actually accepting and living by this ultimate truth, was perplexing as well as exciting for me. This was my connection to my true self; to God and all there is.

It wasn't that I didn't already believe in God, I truly did, although I had many doubts about the validity of organised religions. I had questioned religious belief systems that purported to be the only true religion. Teaching that only their followers would be 'saved' and those without that belief system are somehow doomed! Logic had long ago convinced me that this could not be the case and that somehow the ego of mankind had come between God and God's offspring. The basic premise that 'God is Love' does not account for these divisive belief systems.

My Spiritual journey, however, is something that is hard to describe as it is experiential and much of what I encountered whilst meditating and communicating with Spirit is beyond words. I would describe the experiences as simply having a sense of *coming home*. A feeling of *everything is just as it should be* followed by *it will turn out all right*.

Interestingly, a passing comment my sister said to me one day early in my diagnosis, also helped me to find the *God within*. She told me that I should listen to a song by Neil Diamond called 'Turn on Your Heart Light'. Around this time, my friend Debbie introduced me to a heart meditation, which involved *going into* my heart centre. Those two things together made sense. I listened to the song with tears streaming down my face. I knew that on some level my heart was closed to love. The pure unconditional love of myself, and the love of others. I was completely unaware of this on a mental level. I genuinely thought that I loved myself, as well as others. However, there was still a piece of the jigsaw puzzle missing, and I was about to find out what it was.

The heart meditation involved me going into my heart centre to experience love in all its glory. The feelings are impossible to put into words and therefore difficult to explain. This love is not love as we normally know and understand it to be.

It is pure, unconditional love. It is what I would describe as 'God-love'. The love that comes from God, the God we can find within. Not an external source as many would believe, but our true essence. The pure life force energy within all of us. We are all 'sons and daughters of God' and all a part of the Universal energy of love. Like magic, we can all access this love directly without an intermediary. It is freely given for those who request it. The challenge is that most people do not ask. They live in fear and are unaware of this love. They are ignorant of the truth that God's love will banish the fear because love and fear cannot live side by side simultaneously.

Somewhere between the conscious mind and the subconscious is a place where I was residing much of the time. I have decided to call it 'Knowingland'. This is where the conscious and subconscious meet. It is a place of reflection as well as of action. I was experienced at meditating having done so for many years.

The ancient art of meditation has been extremely valuable to me on many occasions and has allowed me to change the focus of my life from that of a driven individual to one whose primary focus is on experiencing the moment. This is by no means a statement that I am in any way an expert in the art of meditation, whatever that may be, and I know that there is a lot about the power of meditation that I do not as yet understand and experience. I am simply stating that my personal meditation experiences have allowed me to cultivate greater calm in my life.

What my own experience taught me is that I also

had to take consistent corrective action to change my situation. This for me is where the two parts of the conscious meet. Their coming together gave me the inspiration, motivation, and tenacity to carry on, despite the dark days when I struggled to get out of bed to take the girls to school. On those days when it was such an enormous effort to walk the dog or even to make my healthy lunch. Days when I had to lie down and sleep in the afternoon through sheer exhaustion, having done little apart from that.

Knowingland is a bit like Neverland in that the same story repeats itself without fail and the solutions, though varied keep coming and being implemented. With a deep seated belief that 'good will prevail in the end', even when things seem impossible for the characters involved. I was looking upon each day with the same awe and wonder of the child who loves Peter Pan; with an acceptance of the magic that I couldn't really understand or explain. Then little by little the fairy dust would fall, and I would notice my health gradually improving. My skin was softer, even although I no longer lathered masses of moisturiser on it every day. My hair was shinier, and my nails were stronger than they had been in years. Other people noticed the difference too, especially John, which helped to convince him that I was on the right track.

For as long as I can remember I held the belief that *I am not special, I am just ordinary.*

My healing journey has shown me that not only am I special, but I am also wonderful. This knowledge is not ego-driven or designed so that I can stand apart from others who may consider themselves less so. What I know is that everyone is special. God made every one of us, and we are all special and wonderful. This means that what I have done, anyone who chooses a similar path can do too.

As I have said previously, in the short term, it may not seem like the easiest route to take, and there are many unknowns along the way. Holding onto your belief that everything is going to work out needs courage and tenacity. Finding that inside is such a wonderful experience and reaps many rewards. I would never say that others in a similar situation to myself should follow exactly what I did.

There is no 'one size fits all' recipe to follow. However, there are key actions which helped to move me from illness to wellness. Others don't need to do exactly what I did, as we are all unique and each person can adapt the process to find what works for them. In fact, there are so many alternative options to mainstream medicine, part of the process of working out my own unique formula was to decide what I preferred and what fitted in with my lifestyle.

My role is to inspire and not advise. This is something I have had to remind myself of on occasion. It is just so tempting to adopt 'fix it' mode when someone shares their own story.

Upon starting to type up my story, I simply thought *If I am able to inspire at least one person through sharing my story then I know writing this book has been worthwhile.* However, even before I was finished I had begun to share my story, and people began to feel inspired by what I had to say. I genuinely believe that our destiny is in our hands and it is so empowering to take charge of our health and not abdicate responsibility to others for our wellbeing, or for anything else in our life. It may initially seem the easiest path, to allow others to determine our destiny, but this road is fraught with troubles. If things go wrong, blaming others may seem justifiable for a while. This approach will not, however, provide lasting solutions to our health, or life problems.

Even although it is done with the best intentions, trying to tell others what may be able to help them, simply doesn't work. I found this out after I was introduced to Reiki for the first time and wanted to help others discover what a difference it could make to their lives. Interestingly, towards the end of my healing journey, I started to meet others who had been diagnosed with cancer. I wanted to help them, but had to stop myself from trying to solve other people's problems. It is always hard to stand back when you have the knowledge and experience which may help another to feel better, especially when it is someone you know.

Another valuable lesson that I learned is that not everyone is going to like the message I feel compelled to relay. In fact, I know that what I have to say challenges many people's belief system as it links to some of their deepest fears.

I experienced the full force of someone's anger one evening whilst at a friend's birthday party. I didn't know anyone there apart from my friend, so I was happy to chat to a few of her acquaintances. Whilst I was engaged in a conversation with one of her friends whom I seemed to have a lot to chat about, I experienced a challenge which stopped me short. She had been telling me how Tai Chi had helped her with her mobility problems.

Although at this point I hadn't shared my story with many people, I felt it was safe to share what I had done with this lady. The ferocity of her anger felt like a physical blow. I had almost finished a summary of what I had done when she challenged me "what will you do when the cancer comes back?" I was flabbergasted. I replied in a calm and confident voice that I would simply do the same thing again, even though I didn't think that would happen. She then proceeded to question, whilst becoming increasingly agitated "would you not go to hospital if you had a broken arm? You might need doctors and nurses then. What if you were in a car accident?"

I looked at her and smiled. I knew I had to remove

myself from this altercation before I picked up on her anger. I replied, "yes, of course, I would go to the hospital if I had such an emergency." I looked the other way took a deep breath and turned back to her and excused myself. I went to the ladies to take stock of what had just happened and why. I started by sending this lady some distant love to help her to heal from her anger and upset. I decided that I was meant to experience this encounter to prepare me for the reality of what my story could trigger in some people. I said my silent thank you to God for this valuable experience, returned to the party and started dancing. It was time to have some fun. I then enjoyed the remainder of the evening.

Although you may be thinking, as others have done, that I was simply caught up in a fairy tale or fantasy, I can assure you that is where the analogy ends. Knowingland does have the magic, however, that magic is real and of this world. The good news is that it is freely available to anyone who desires it. It is not just for a 'chosen few'. It is for everyone to tap into and to share. This magic is, in essence, God's love and it is freely given to all who ask for it. You need no special introductions, no rituals nor intermediaries, and no religion. It is a free, open and endless channel to our source. What I am not saying is that it is necessarily easy, however, it's not difficult either. It is simply what you want it to be. We all choose our own path. In choosing, you are never restricted and can simply change your course at any time. There are no rules, and there are no boundaries. You simply need to let go and fly.......

No one likes a story without an 'ending' as such, and I can almost hear many of you thinking, 'What happened next?'

I believe endings are, in effect, new beginnings in the circle of life. Things merely change, they never reach a conclusion - even death is not the end. Therefore, the story always continues for all of us, through triumph and tragedy. Reviewing and renewing as we move forward day by day.

As for me, I am continuing my healthy eating quest, amending, refining and altering my diet as time goes on with the same basic premise that the more natural, organic and unprocessed foods I eat the better it is for me. My research continues, and each day I learn more about myself and my needs, physically, mentally, emotionally and of course spiritually. Where I can, I simply take one moment at a time one day at a time.

I learned, and am still learning to integrate my heightened spiritual awareness into my life because I truly am a 'spiritual being having a human experience'. Which at times can be difficult. I have been known to say out loud, to no one in particular, "this being human is hard sometimes". Simply by acknowledging and vocalising this observation, somehow makes any situation, even the most challenging, feel better. It's not really what happens to us in life that defines us; it is what we do as a result.

Just because my body healed itself, does not mean that all my troubles have gone. I am still very much on the journey of life with its ups and downs. As in the words of Jack Kornfield when he refers to the Buddha's life and teachings. 'We are not trying to get somewhere better next year or in twenty years... We are learning to open to the timeless unfurling of our lives, being in greater and greater harmony with what is, with a greater inclusiveness of our hearts to all the seasons of our life.' [38]

In doing this, I have been able to develop my business to treat more clients and run more courses. My Spiritual Group also grew, enabling more people to connect with like-minded individuals and discuss their spirituality and where they are on their spiritual path. Then one day I realised that it was time to move on. I found this difficult as this group of people had been with me throughout my healing journey. They had shared the laughter and the tears. I knew I had to embrace the change. Moving on to what I did not know, however I was prepared to be led by my intuition. The same intuition which served me well during my healing journey.

I am especially thankful for all the moral support and help I received from the few friends and family members who knew about my diagnosis and supported me on my alternative path. To them, I say "Namaste". I continue to be grateful for all the joys, may they be large or small, in my life. The words of encouragement from friends, family, and strangers.

I continue to work on loving myself and enjoying the moment. Being thankful for life and all it brings. The variety, the experiences, the love, the beauty and the people who enter my life as teachers, they are all special. I love and appreciate them all for who they are in this moment, not seeking to change or alter them in any way. Just being thankful for their presence in my life. These are things that I will always do. They have become part of my purpose, part of my reason for being, part of my life path. I am thankful for them all.

I now wish to inspire others with my story and to tell them that, "Yes, I am special, and so are you." I honestly believe that anyone can do what I have done. I know from experience that surrender is infinitely easier than fighting. I send you all my love and blessings for a happy and healthy life.

This story is not just about healing from cancer, nor any other disease for that matter. Perhaps it will help inspire you and your loved ones to take a wider view of illness and healing. However, it is also a story about life and life lessons. It is a story about taking charge of yourself and being in control of your own destiny. For those who wish to be in 'the driving seat' of their own lives, I say "Yes you can!"

Where I journey next, will not be without its challenges I am sure. I believe we are here to face those trials head-on and deal with them to help us develop spiritually. I know I still have a lot to learn, as well as to share. I am grateful to you for reading my story, and I sincerely hope that my words have moved you to help yourself and others towards a brighter future.

END

Visit Rhona's website - www.rhonabyrne.co.uk

Email: rhona@rhonabyrne.co.uk

Bibliography

Some of these books give me practical ideas to help on my healing journey, and others simply helped to inspire me.

"Cancer is not a Disease" Andreas Moritz

"You Are What You Eat" Gillian McKeith

"Say No to Cancer" Patrick Holford

"Mum's NOT having chemo" Laura Bond

"The Journey" Brandon Bays

"The Miracle of Mindfulness" Jon Kabbat-Zinn

"The Secrets of 100% Healthy People" Patrick Holford

"The Gerson Therapy: the Proven Nutritional Program for Cancer and Other Illnesses" Charlotte Gerson and Morton Walker D.P.M.

"True Happiness" Dr. Mark Atkinson

"The Optimum Nutrition Bible" Patrick Holford

"A Path with Heart" Jack Kornfield

"The Biology of Belief" Bruce H. Lipton, PhD

"A Return to Love" Marianne Williamson

"The Power of Intention" Dr. Wayne W. Dyer

"I Can See Clearly Now" Dr. Wayne W. Dyer

"There is a Spiritual Solution to Every Problem" Dr. Wayne W. Dyer

"Mirror Work" Louise Hay

"Why Kindness if Good For You" David R. Hamilton PhD

"The Truth About Cancer" Ty M. Bollinger

"A New Earth" Eckhart Tolle

References

1   Ty M. Bollinger "The Truth About Cancer"
Pages 122-123

2   Andreas Moritz "Cancer is NOT a Disease"
page vii

3   Andreas Moritz "Cancer is NOT a Disease"
Page 41

4   Dr Wayne W. Dyer "There is a Spiritual
Solution to Every Problem"
Page 213

5   Andreas Moritz " Cancer is NOT a Disease"
Page 130

6   Andres Moritz " Cancer is NOT a Disease"
Page 128

7   Andres Moritz " Cancer is NOT a Disease"
Page 100

8   Dolores Cannon from Dolores Cannon.com
(About)

9   Dr David Hamilton "Why Kindness is Good
For You"
Page 168

10   Brandon Bays "The Journey"
Pages 10 & 11

11   Brandon Bays "The Journey"
Page 28

12   Brandon Bays "The Journey"
        Page 76

13   Patrick Holford "Say no to Cancer"
        Pages 123-132

14   Ty M Bollinger ""The TRUTH about CANCER"
        Pages 114-115 & 152

15   Patrick Holford "Say no to Cancer"
        Pages 182-183

16   Andreas Moritz " Cancer is NOT a Disease"
        Page 131

17   Patrick Holford "Say no to Cancer"
        Page 99

18   Gillian McKeith "You Are What You Eat"
        Pages 202-214

19   Patrick Holford "Say No To Cancer"
        Page118

20   Patrick Holford "Say no to Cancer"
        Page 277

21   Omura Y, Beckman SL "Role of mercury
        (Hg) in resistant infections & effective
        treatment of Chlamydia trachomatis and
        Herpes family viral infections (and potential
        treatment for cancer) by removing localized
        Hg deposits with Chinese parsley and
        delivering effective antibiotics using various
        drug uptake enhancement methods."
        Acupunct Electrother Res. 1995 Aug-

Dec;20(3-4):195-229. Heart Disease
Research Foundation, New York, USA.

22   Ty M. Bollinger "The TRUTH about CANCER"
      Page 249

23   Ty M. Bollinger "The TRUTH about CANCER"
      Page 252

24   Patrick Holford "Say no to Cancer"
      Page 258

25   Ty M. Bollinger "The TRUTH about CANCER"
      Page 116

26   Patrick Holford "Say no to Cancer"
      Page 278-279

27   Patrick Holford "Say no to Cancer"
      Page 56

28   Laura Bond "Mum's NOT having chemo"
      Page 268

29   Ty M. Bollinger "The TRUTH about CANCER"
      Pages 160-165

30   Laura Bond "Mum's NOT having chemo"
      Pages 83-98

31   Charlotte Gerson and Morton Walker D.P.M.
      "The Gerson Therapy: the Proven Nutritional
      Program for Cancer and Other Illnesses"

32   Laura Bond "Mum's NOT having chemo"
      Pages 83

33   Laura Bond "Mum's NOT having chemo"
      Pages 82-101

34   Laura Bond "Mum's NOT having chemo"
      Pages 88-89

35   Ty M. Bollinger "The TRUTH about CANCER"
      Pages 108-109

36   AN INTERVIEW WITH TAKATA-SENSEI, MAY
      17, 1975 MRS. TAKATA OPENS MINDS TO
      'REIKI'
      by Vera Graham
      (Printed in 'The Times', San Mateo,
      California).

37   Eckhart Tolle "A New Earth"
      Page 96

38   Jack Kornfield "A Path with Heart"
      Page 182